April 6, 1999

To Bob Hammel,

from

Margaret Sash

The Iron Man From Indiana

The Don Lash Story

By Don Lash

Publishers Turner®

Turner Publishing Company
Publishers of America's History
P.O. Box 3101
Paducah, Kentucky 42002-3101

Co-published by Turner Publishing Company
and Mark A. Thompson, Associate Publisher

Pre-Press work by M. T. Publishing Company, Inc.
Graphic Designers: Rachel NaVille and Elizabeth Dennis

Copyright © 1999
Margaret M. Lash

This book or any part thereof may not be reproduced without the written consent of the Publishers and Margaret M. Lash.

The materials were compiled and produced using available information; Turner Publishing Company and M. T. Publishing Company, Inc. regret they cannot assume liability for errors or omissions.

Author: Don Lash

Library of Congress Catalog
Card No. 98-61816

ISBN: 1-56311-493-3

Printed in the United States of America

Limited Edition

Contents

"The Iron Man From Indiana"
The Don Lash Story

Preface	4
Athletic Career	6
Early Childhood	7
Indiana University	10
1936 Olympics	13
The James E. Sullivan Award	14
Indoor Track	16
Social Life	17
Graduation And Marriage	18
Indiana State Police	19
Life In The Federal Bureau Of Investigation	19
Camp Wapello	25
Methodist Family Of The Year	32
Fellowship Of Christian Athletes	32
Reflections On The Indiana General Assembly	34
Retirement	38
Auburn, Indiana	38
Closing Thoughts	39
Stories, Letters, And Speeches	41
Index	71

Preface

Some people may remember the name of Don Lash from my early years in athletics, when I broke world records, made the U.S. Olympic Team in the 5,000 and 10,000 meters, and was National Cross Country Champion for seven consecutive years. Many of these achievements happened while I was a student at Indiana University in the 1930s.

My athletic career at Indiana University was only the first stage of my life. From there I went into the Indiana State Police for three years, then into the Federal Bureau of Investigation for twenty-one years, and from which I retired. While still in the F.B.I., I started to build a camp for young people in Parke County, Indiana. After retiring from the Bureau, I went with the Fellowship of Christian Athletes for ten years, was a member of the Board of Trustees of Indiana University for two years, and resigned to run for the Indiana State Legislature. I was a State Representative for ten years until I was forced to retire because of my heart. I then gave my time to the Don Lash Realtors in Rockville, Indiana, which I had founded earlier.

Athletics gave me the confidence to undertake accomplishments that seemed impossible to others. I did not do these deeds alone; God helped me all through my life and it is to Him that I give the credit.

My motto for life has been:

The older I become, the more I am convinced that true happiness comes from helping others.

The Iron Man From Indiana
The Don Lash Story

While it is true that I was famous as an athlete and, in the words of *Sports Illustrated* (December 12, 1988), was the "first great distance runner in America", this is only a part of my life story. I was a strong runner and, because of this, my coach at Indiana University, E.C.(Billy) Hayes, would have me run two or more races in the same evening and then maybe anchor a relay team. Thus, the New York Sports Writers called me "The Iron Man From Indiana". I knew that I had a strong body and often proved the sports writers correct. The University also believed this and my Cross Country coach, Sid Robinson, who was at the time working to complete his Doctorate Degree in the Physiology of Exercises, would often have me run on the treadmill to see just how far I could run. Sid would keep track of my heart rate during these tests and note how much blood my heart was pumping. I was told that, when I was running my best, my heart was pumping blood at the equivalent of four water faucets turned on full force at the same time. After I broke the Two Mile Indoor World Record at Boston in 1937, Coach Robinson and Dr. Dill of Harvard University grabbed me and pulled me under the bleachers to take my heart rate and my blood count. I was always willing to cooperate on these tests for I wanted to know these facts for myself.

I believe that the idea that I was an "Iron Man" influenced my life. My wife often said that never in our 56 years of married life did I ever admit to being tired. Never in athletics, never after working all day to build our camp while cutting trees, hauling gravel, or hauling heavy stones up from the canyon did I ever admit to being tired. It was never in my vocabulary to say that I was tired.

Athletic Career

Of course my athletic career started earlier than my days at Indiana University. It started in Auburn, Indiana in high school. My older brother, Charles, was a good athlete in football, basketball, and track. His coach, "Zeke" Young, expected me to follow in his footsteps, but I did not like contact sports, especially football. I could see no point in knocking someone down, his getting up and then knocking me down. I liked basketball better, but I really liked track and cross country where I could run out in the open. So "Zeke" encouraged me in this sport. I won several ribbons in high school, and I won the State Championship in the Mile and Half-Mile races in my senior year in high school. This was when my name became known in sports annals.

After graduating from Indiana University and getting married, I took a job with the Indiana State Police where I continued to run in the big meets in New York and Boston. I did most of my police work as a speaker and public relations man. I spoke mostly to schools and service clubs on athletics and clean living. Some days I would have four speaking engagements in one day. I managed to do some police work and at the same time finished my Master's Degree in Police Science at the University. At IU, I had prepared to teach and be a coach, but during my last semester as a senior, they offered a course in Police Science and, since I had been the victim of a robbery one evening, I was interested in police work. It worked out well, too, for I was able to run down a few criminals in later years, much to their surprise.

After three years as an Indiana State Policeman, I applied for and was accepted into the Federal Bureau of Investigation as an Agent under J. Edgar Hoover. This was the end of my athletic career, because, as an Agent of the F.B.I., I could not be effective if I were identified. I enjoyed running and keeping physically fit by joining the Y.M.C.A. and using their facilities whenever possible. A daily workout was important to me. I did get permission from Mr. Hoover to try for the Olympics in 1948. However, I dropped out of the Olympic trials in Milwaukee because of the heat and humidity.

In 1961 I returned to Indiana University, where Dr. Robinson and Dr. Dill again put me on a treadmill as part of their study to follow up on athletes after competition. Results indicated that my heart rate remained the same as tests made in the 1930's.

I had done well in athletics but now it was time to do other things with my life. I felt that God had plans for me other than athletics. I, as a result of athletics: 1) Broke world records in the two-mile run, indoors and outdoors; 2) Anchored medley and four-mile relay teams to world records; 3) Was the first American to run two-miles in under nine minutes; 4) Won the National Cross Country Champion for seven consecutive years, a record that stood for over fifty years; 5) Was a member of the

1936 U.S. Olympic Team to Berlin, competing in the 5,000 and 10,000 meter events; 6) Held every national record from 3,000 to 10,000 meters in 1935, 1936 and 1937; 7) Received the James E. Sullivan Award in 1938 as the "Most Outstanding Amateur Athlete in the United States"; 8) Was inducted into the U.S. Track Hall of Fame; 9) Was inducted into the A.A.U. Track & Field Hall of Fame; 10)Was inducted into the Indiana Track Hall of Fame; 11) Became a charter member of Indiana University Hall of Fame. I felt it was time to move on from athletics and, at the same time, devote more of my time to God, my country, and my family. I became an Agent of the F.B.I. and took on the duties of defending my country as war clouds were thickening in 1941.

Early Childhood

I was born in Bluffton, Indiana, the third child of Brandon and Pearl Lash. My father worked in the Red Cross Foundry as a molder in Bluffton. Later he moved his family to Auburn, Indiana where he worked at the Auburn Cord Foundry as a specialty molder. When there was a call for a broken part and there was no mold for it, Brandon was called to hand mold a piece for the broken part so the machinery could be fixed.

My father, Brandon, had an unusual background. He was born in Massachusetts and, after his mother died, he was placed in an orphan's home at the age of eight. After about one year, he was placed on an Orphan Train that was heading west to find homes in the Midwest farm belt with caring, loving families. Brandon was taken to raise by Charles and Anna Lash of Bluffton, Indiana. They were a Christian couple with no children. Charles and Anna had a small 65-acre farm on which they raised strawberries, grain, chickens and a few pigs. Charles wanted a boy to help him with the strawberries. They took Brandon and gave him all the love and schooling that they could give. He was happy with them, but after the "trial year", Charles decided to give him back to the Orphan's Home, because he decided Brandon was too small for farm chores. But Brandon ran to his "Mother" and put his arms around her and begged her not to send him back to the orphan's home. She prevailed and he stayed with them.

As Brandon grew to manhood, he met a young girl who lived nearby named Pearl Landis. They fell in love and married. The story is told about my Dad, Brandon, that on the day of his wedding went rabbit hunting. He claimed to have shot forty rabbits that morning. Maybe true- maybe exaggerated- but it was his story.

Pearl's father, Daniel Landis, was a farmer and preacher in the Church of the Brethren. One day while farming, Daniel caught his hand in the thrashing machine and lost his hand. I always remember him as a small man with a hook for a hand. Pearl had two sisters and three brothers. They moved to Michigan and I only saw them occasionally at family reunions. Brandon was an only child and thus his family consisted of my grandparents, Charles and Anna Lash.

Brandon and Pearl's family grew while they lived in Auburn until there were six children. Charles and I were the only boys with four sisters. We took great delight in teasing the girls for we had no other form of entertainment. We especially liked to tease our older sister, Josephine, when her boyfriends came to call on her. We teased the younger ones also, but not as much as Josephine. I remember one time that I hid behind the couch and listened to their conversation and then repeated it at the supper table with all of the family present.

Earlier when I was about six to eight years old, I liked to go out to my grandparent's (Charles and Anna's) home near Bluffton and spend the summers. They had a fox terrier dog named "Bob" and a horse named "Mary" who pulled the buggy. Bob was my best friend and we would go hunting together. My grandfather would hitch Mary to the buggy and we would go into town for groceries. While there he would give me 25 cents to go to the hardware store and buy shells for his rifle. Then Bob and I would hunt squirrels and rabbits. When it came time to harvest the wheat, Bob and I would watch the binder go round, and as the field got smaller and smaller, the young rabbits would run out. Bob and I would run and catch them and I would put them into a pen. After they grew and got fatter, we would have rabbit for supper. I always said this was where I first learned to run: on Grandpa's farm catching rabbits. One time I killed a bird and my Grandma was horrified. She was sure that I was destined for a life of crime. However, it was all right with her to shoot a squirrel or rabbit that we could eat.

One time Bob kept barking at something under the barn. Grandpa couldn't see what it was, but I could. It was a skunk. Bob knew what it was, too, and wouldn't tangle with it. But I, mischievous as I was, said, "Sic-em, Bob", and obedient Bob did just that! He went under the barn and got the skunk! Of course the skunk gave him a "full blast", and poor Bob rolled in the grass and dirt and scooted on the ground to get rid of the odor. I really felt ashamed of myself for doing that to my best friend.

I always slept in a room upstairs while my grandparents slept downstairs. One night I was awakened to see a very bright light in front of me in my bedroom. We had no electric lights or other lights around. The light moved to the right of the room and then to the left, back and forth. I was scared and started to scream for my Grandpa. He, of course, got up, lighted a lamp and came up the stairs. By the time he got upstairs the light disappeared. There was no explanation for it, except that I have always believed that God was telling me that I was a chosen one of His.

Later, when I was nine years old until I was eighteen, my family lived in Auburn during the winter months but would move out into the country and rent a muck farm for the summer months. Muck farms were good for raising potatoes, onions and celery. We raised potatoes and onions for these crops needed to be weeded by hand and we children could do this. My father still worked at the foundry in Auburn and would come home in the evening and inspect to see how much work we had done during the day. We called him "The Inspector".

It was my job to plow the fields with a one-horse plow. I will always remember that my father would put a handkerchief on a stick at the far end of the field and tell me to line up the horses' ears on either side of that marker and my rows would be straight. That was a good lesson for me for life: "set your goal and work hard to realize it".

This crop of potatoes and onions helped our family income for we raised lots of them and sold them wholesale. When fall came and we sold our crop, we would move back to Auburn and we children would attend Auburn schools. There were times in late spring and early fall when we attended schools in the country. I remember one school was a one room school where all eight grades were in one room and we had to walk to school which was about two miles from our home.

Charles and I had paper routes to help on the family income. We carried the Auburn Star and the Saturday Evening Post. My mother was a hard worker. She not only took care of our family but also took in washings and cleaned houses for people. She was also a very religious person and saw to it that everyone in the family was scrubbed on Saturday night and dressed in their best clothes for Sunday school and church on Sunday morning. She herself was at Sunday evening service and Wednesday night prayer service. She was very influential in the family's Christian upbringing, probably due to her father's influence as a preacher. At one of those evening services, I went forward to give my life to God. She was sitting in the back of the church, but said she knew it was me because she could see my red toboggan hat.

We did not have money to spend for entertainment but we were a strong family with lots of fun, trials and tears. I always kept things interesting by teasing my sisters and my dad. Dad frequently threatened to "lick" me but never did.

My father didn't go too far in school. I don't think he went any further than high school and I don't think my mother even went that far. However they were pretty learned people and knew how to make a living in tight spots... they had to many times for our family back in the 1920's and 1930's.

At Auburn High School we did not have a track for our team. Outdoors we ran in a man's pasture and on the inside, in bad weather, we ran in the school building. Since our school was a two-story building with an attic our coach, Zeke Young, would have us start in the gym, run upstairs to the second floor, run up another stairs to the attic, down both flights of stairs and into the gym again. We ran this course until Zeke thought we had had a good workout. This gave us a pretty good workout, and, of course, this was done after school.

When I was in the 8th grade I began to run a little and Zeke began to notice me. When I got into high school, Zeke was the football, basketball and track coach. Charles was a good football and basketball player and Zeke thought I would also be good in those sports. However, as I said earlier, I did not like contact sports where someone would knock me down and then I would knock them down. I liked basketball better, but I really liked to run. I became a better runner than Charles and soon Zeke let me run in place of playing football or basketball. When I was a senior in high school, I was one of three boys on the Auburn track team that would win almost every meet we entered. Zeke took us to the state track meet and we won. I won the state championship in the mile and half mile races. That is when my name began to be known in the track world.

Indiana University

As a family, we did not have any extra money and we always just seemed to squeeze through each situation. We had all pulled together to send my older brother, Charles, to Purdue University. I had saved some money for college and then one of my sisters had to have an emergency operation so I gave my money to her. Therefore, when it came time for me to go to college, I had no money. I traveled to Indiana University and talked to Coach E.C. (Billy) Hayes. I found out there was a scholarship at Auburn High School that no one had claimed and I could use the money for my tuition. Coach Hayes said, "Well, we'll get you a job around here and start in and see how it goes". When it came time for me to go to I.U., I went to my dad for some money. He said, "I'll give you all I have", and he pulled out $4.75 from his pocket. So I started out with that amount. The man who allowed me to ride down to the university at Bloomington with his son charged me $2.00 for the ride. I'm sure he did not know the predicament in which it left me. At the end of the first week, I went in to talk with Coach Hayes and told him that I was going to have to go home for I was out of money and hungry. He told me to go over to his house and water the lawn. When I finished he gave me $10.00. In the mean time, he had called the lady in charge of the girl's dormitories and kitchens where some of the other track men had jobs. She promised me two meals a day if I would mop the kitchens and dining rooms. That was fine for I did not eat lunch in order to have time for a workout in the afternoon. One of the fraternities, the Delta Chi's, gave me a bed just to say that they had good athletes at their house. They already

Breaking world record in
two mile run at Princeton University.

Don Lash with trophies in senior year
at Indiana University

had two All-American football players at their house and needed a track man. I also got a job with the Beech Nut Chewing Gum Company to pass out samples of gum at the sorority and fraternity houses and at the dormitories for $10.00 per week. This is the way that I was able to stay in school.

Of course I had quite a career in the world of track. I broke the world's record in the two-mile run indoors and outdoors; was within a second of setting the world's record in the mile run; was national champion in cross country for seven consecutive years (a record that stood for over fifty years); anchored the I.U. teams in the medley and four-mile teams to world's records; and, as noted previously, *Sports Illustrated* credited me with being the "first great distance runner in America." I don't know that that was necessarily true, however, at the time, I was probably the best. I broke Paavo Nurmi's records. He was the great Finnish runner. You don't hear much about him now but, at that time, he was a tremendous runner and to break his records was something else!

As I became a better athlete, I was invited to track meets in New York City and Boston. I was able to save a little money on these trips. The promoters were not allowed to pay the athletes but they did have to give them first class transportation and meals. I would ride the day coach from Indianapolis to Pittsburgh, then get a sleeper. On the ride home, I would ride the day coach all the way. Thus I could save $30.00 on a trip to New York. This also helped me pay my way through Indiana University.

In June of 1936 I was invited to Princeton University for a track meet. This was an invitational meet and only a few good athletes were invited to participate. Coach Hayes had scheduled me to compete in the two mile, because he wanted me to break Paavo Nurmi's world record that had stood for several years. I was to run each lap at a specified time and in doing so would break the record. When I got up on the morning of the race, it was raining. My spirits fell for I thought it impossible to win on a soggy track. Coach Hayes knew what I was thinking and convinced me that the rain was good. "It will just cool you off", he said. So I did as he said, and, sure enough, when I crossed the finish line, I had broken Nurmi's record!

1936 Olympics

After the race at Princeton, I prepared for the Olympic Trials which were to be in meters instead of miles. I had to run the distance races of 5,000 and 10,000 meters to qualify for the Olympics. The trials were held at Randall's Island in New York City. My team mate, Tommy Deckard and I were both going to try to make the team. Tommy often beat me in practice, but, in the big races, I usually won. I had won the race in the 10,000 meters and was assured of a place on the Olympic team. Tommy had not made the team, but I felt he could make it in the 5,000 meter race. Only the first three runners could make the team. I was leading the race in the 5,000 meter run when I looked back and saw Tommy in the back of the pack. I slowed my pace until I got back with Tommy and said: "Come on, Tommy, you can do it ... just stay with me." Tommy did and when he'd followed me up to third place so he could make the team, I sprinted ahead and just caught Zamperini at the tape. The New York sports fans thought something was wrong with me when I slowed down, but, when I sprinted ahead and won the race, they realized I had dropped back to encourage my team mate. Thus Tommy and I both went to Berlin for the 1936 Olympics.

Everyone expected me to do great things in Berlin after just setting a world record at Princeton; however, this was not how things turned out. The U.S. team went to Berlin via boat, the *Manhattan*, and it took ten days to cross the Atlantic. To a runner this was disastrous. To be in good condition, I needed a daily workout but I could not run on the boat because of the motion of the waves. If I had tried to run I would have gotten shin splints, thus I had no workouts for ten days. There was plenty of food and athletes are notoriously hungry. Because I could not workout, I gained weight even though I ate no more than usual. But the worst was yet to come when I learned that my races were scheduled for the first two days after we landed and I had no time to get back in condition. As a result, I placed back in the field in both races. I consoled myself by saying that I would come back in 1940 and win these races. This was not to be for war was imminent and the 1940 Olympics were canceled. Thus my dream to win an Olympic gold medal vanished.

The James E. Sullivan Award

I had gone to New Orleans to run in the Sugar Bowl Track Meet which was held the day before the Sugar Bowl Football Game on New Years Day. The officials asked me to stay over for the football game which I agreed to do. At the half time intermission, they brought me down to center field and announced that I was the winner of the James E. Sullivan Award for athletic achievement and sportsmanship for the year of 1938. This is the most prestigious award in amateur athletics. The trophy was presented to me later at the New York Athletic Club on a trip to New York City. My trophy is now on loan to the Indiana State Museum in Indianapolis. I prize it above all of my trophies and wish it to be on display so that others may see it at the museum. The sports officials named my act of helping my team mate, Tommy Deckard, to make the Olympic team as the reason for my being selected for this award. This along with my world records and winning two events on the Olympic team convinced the judges that I was worthy of this distinguished honor.

Don Lash receiving Sullivan Award.

Indoor Track

Indoor track was different from outdoor track. The races were run on boards and I had to adjust my stride to the vibration of the boards. It took some time to master the board track, however the big track meets in the winter were in New York City's Madison Square Garden and the Boston Garden. Therefore if I ran in these meets, I had to learn to run on the boards.

I always liked to run in Boston for I knew that my father's natural parents had lived in Massachusetts and I felt that I was running for them. One night at a meet in Boston in the winter of 1937 my coach had signed me up to run the mile race and the two mile race. I knew that Glen Cunningham, who held the world record in the mile run, would also be running and probably win this this race. I didn't want to get beat by Glen, so I went to my coach and begged off from running the mile race saying that I didn't feel well. My coach knew what was bothering me: I didn't want to run against Glen. The next thing I heard was the announcer saying "Lash has scratched from the mile race to concentrate on a new world record in the two mile race." If you think I felt sick before, you should have seen how sick I felt after that announcement! I went off by myself and prayed. As I looked up into the stands, I could sense God's comfort with the words from Psalm 121: "I will lift up mine eyes unto the hills from whence my help cometh..." God heard my prayer that night and helped me. I broke the world indoor record in the two-mile race with Gods help.

One time our team was to run in the Penn Relays. In those days we traveled by car, and Coach Hayes would let one of the boys drive. We were driving pretty fast and the driver lost control. We rolled end over end and then down an embankment and landed safely between two telephone poles. Surprisingly enough, no one was injured. After the athletes got themselves out of the car, they righted it, piled back into the car, and proceeded on to the relays. God certainly was with us that day!

They used to give medals and loving cups and different things as trophies when we won a race. I remember that at the Penn Relays that day I won four gold watches. I had won in the 5,000 and 10,000 meter races, the four mile relay and the medley relay. In those days, I was the anchor man for the relays. Jimmy Smith, Tommy Deckard, Mel Trutt and I usually made up those relay teams. We all got gold watches of course, but I had four of them in one day! I kept all those watches for some time, but I don't know where they are now.

Coach Hayes was a special coach. He not only coached the boys in athletics but also directed their lives. He checked their grades, their grammar, their social lives and, above all, their girlfriends. He seemed to know all about each athlete...even their diets. He used to tell us to stop eating whenever dry bread did not taste good. It was important that runners not put on weight and this was his method of keeping us in shape. I guess my girlfriend (and wife-to-be), Margaret, passed his inspection for he heartily approved of her!

Social Life

At this point I have said little about my social life or my spiritual life, and I would like to say a few words about this. As already indicated, I had one of the best coaches in the world in Billy Hayes. He knew all about his athletes, who they were dating, what courses they were taking, what they were doing and everything else. I think he knew more about me than I did myself since I was one of his top athletes. As a whole, he didn't have to worry about me, I don't think, because I was bashful and I didn't go out with the girls. I remember when I was a member of the Delta Chi Fraternity they had a rule that you had to go to the Delta Chi Dance and that meant you had to have a date with a girl. Well, I wasn't going because, first, I didn't want to go and, second, I didn't have a date. Our fraternity president, Jim Lease from Petersburg, Indiana, said, "Don you're going to go to the dance!" I said, "I don't have a date!" Jim said, "Oh yes you do! You're going to go and take my girl!" I said, "Take your girl?" Jim just smiled and confided, "Yes, Don, you are one of a few that I would trust to take my girl to the dance!" And that is how I ended up going to the dance with someone else's girlfriend!

While several young coeds always seemed anxious to get a date with an athlete, I don't think I had a date at Indiana University until I met Margaret. In the fall of 1936, I was a junior at IU and had just returned from the Olympics. The first time I saw this pretty dark-haired freshman on the campus, I wondered, "Who is she?" Then one day I saw her go into the girl's dormitory where I had my meals and mopped floors. I asked one of the helpers there who she was and they said, "She's Charlotte Mendenhall's little sister from Pendleton, Indiana!" Charlotte had been a student at IU and had lived at Memorial Hall. She had dropped out that year when Margaret came to the campus. I wanted to get a date with Margaret, but I was bashful. Finally, I enlisted the aid of a track team friend, Sam Miller. Sam seemed to know her better than anyone, so I asked him if he would present her with a package of one of my Beech Nut gum samples and tell her it was from me. Sam said he would. After delivering my gift, Sam came straight back and told me that when he had given it to her and told her that it was from Don Lash, she asked, "Who's Don Lash?" At that time I was well known by everyone on the IU campus, and apparently the girls around her chided her for not knowing my name! But that didn't matter to me, I was just glad to get to know her. And, as it turned out, Margaret was everything I had ever dreamed about! She was not only pretty, but, as I have often said, she was soft as a kitten. Moreover, in areas where I was weak she was strong. For example in bookkeeping, writing and spelling, she was strong, and I was very weak. I loved her so much and we got along so well, it just seemed that God planned for us to be together. Spiritually, I know that it wasn't I who picked her out for me, but God!

Graduation And Marriage

In June of 1938, I graduated from Indiana University with a B.S. Degree in Physical Education and Police Science. I had applied for and was accepted into the Indiana State Police. Their training school started the next Monday after my graduation. I had planned to run in the Princeton Invitational Meet at Princeton, New Jersey, so Margaret and I used that trip as a means of going to New York City for our wedding. I had three medals with a diamond in each that I had won previously in the Chicago Relays, and a jeweler near the Bloomington campus incorporated them into a wedding ring for Margaret. We were to be married in the afternoon of June 18, 1938 in the Little Church Around the Corner in New York City. Several friends and family members had traveled a long distance to witness our vows, however, the time came and went for our afternoon ceremony, and Margaret and I were no were to be found! Due to a delay in the track and train schedules, instead of repeating our vows at the church, we were standing in the Princeton railroad station! In desperation, I frantically called the preacher and told him what had happened, but as I was speaking to him, the train came rolling into the station. I literally dropped the receiver, grabbed Margaret's hand and we dashed for the train to take us to New York City. By this time, however, our guests at the church assumed we had played a hoax on them and left! When we arrived at 8:00 pm for our wedding, we found that the only ones who had waited for us were members of the media (who were still hoping for a photo), the preacher, and a janitor! The janitor and the photographers served as our witnesses! We came back from New York on the train, and I entered the Indiana State Police Training program the following Monday morning.

Margaret spent the next few weeks buying furniture and making our little house into a home. It was on Sunrise Drive in Bloomington, Indiana, and we called it "Honeymoon Cottage on Sunrise Drive". With four rooms, a well in the backyard and an outside toilet, it certainly wasn't fancy, but it was all we could afford for $15.00 per month. I didn't get a pay check from the State Police until October and then it was $92.00 per month. However, our little house was "Home Sweet Home" to us!

In the fall of 1939, we were expecting our first child. The doctor had said the baby would arrive on Christmas Day. I was expected to run in the Sugar Bowl Meet which was run the day before the Sugar Bowl Football Game and was always held on New Years Day in New Orleans. The papers came out with headlines, "LASH WILL RUN IN SUGAR BOWL MEET IF STORK ARRIVES ON TIME". Glen Cunningham and Archie San Romani had been blessed with little girls, and it was expected that our first baby would also be a girl. However, it seemed as if our lives were full of surprises, and, about noon on Christmas Day, Margaret presented me with a bouncing baby boy. I named him "Russell" after my fraternity-brother-doctor who delivered him and and "Earl" after my coach Earl C. Hayes. Thus he was named Russell Earl Lash. Since the baby arrived on schedule, I was able to run in the Sugar Bowl Meet, much to the relief of the track officials in New Orleans!

Indiana State Police

I was in the State Police for three years. They allowed me to continue running, and I was able to save a little money on each trip to New York and Boston to supplement our income. Much of my work was giving speeches to schools and service clubs. I was also able to finish my Master's Degree at the university, as well as doing some police work. It was Coach Hayes who suggested I apply for a position with the Federal Bureau of Investigation (F.B.I.). I took his advice, and then went to Washington D.C. for a three-month training program to be an F.B.I. Agent.

While I was in Washington D.C., Margaret stayed with her parents in Pendleton, Indiana with Russell. It was during this period that our second baby was born. God blessed us with another boy and Margaret named him David Ray Lash. I was determined that neither boy be named Donald Lash for I felt that it would put a handicap on him to have the same name as his father. David was five weeks old before I came to Pendleton to see him. I had finished my training in the Bureau and was assigned to the Atlanta, Georgia office. After I located a house in Atlanta, Margaret's father brought her and our two little boys to Georgia. Again, we had a home.

Life In The Federal Bureau of Investigation
Atlanta, Georgia

Everything about my assignment in the F.B.I. was new to me, from living in a southern city to the rules of the Bureau. These were stressful days for us in the Bureau, because war clouds were gathering and we were looking for German spies before the attack by the Japanese on Pearl Harbor.

One of my most memorable cases during my F.B.I. career was in Atlanta. Another Agent and I were assigned to search the room of a known German spy who was in the city. We got into the man's room and were photographing everything when word came over the intercom that the man was approaching. We were told to leave immediately. At that moment, I spied a small black notebook. I opened it and recognized names and numbers written in German. Against the orders of my Special Agent In Charge (S.A.C.) not to touch anything, I shoved the notebook into my pocket and we fled. My S.A.C. exploded when I told him about the notebook and said, "Lash, you'll never make an Agent because you can't follow orders!" However, the Bureau went ahead and photographed each page of the confiscated material. It turned out to be the names and addresses of many German spies in this country and was invaluable to the Bureau. The other Agent and I were instructed the next morning to go back to the man's room and return the notebook. This was a dangerous assignment, and we were concerned the spy might have become suspicious and set a trap for us. However, God was with us again, and the mission was successfully accomplished. The very next day war was declared, and the German spy was arrested.

Louisville, Kentucky

Our next office was in Louisville. While there I had another interesting case which involved a crime on a government reservation. It started when a man walked into the Veterans Hospital to visit a friend. He noticed that, as the patients came in, they put their possessions in an envelope. The envelope was then placed near the vault in the office until the patients were released. This man was a criminal, and he and two of his buddies decided this would be a good place to rob. As they committed the robbery, someone saw them and called the police. When the police captured them later, the robbers did not have the loot with them. The F.B.I. was called in because it was a government hospital. We surveyed the situation and determined that the suspects had probably gotten rid of the evidence somewhere along the street before the police picked them up. Another Agent and I decided that the most likely place for them to throw it was down a sewer along the street. We had the sanitation department pump out the sewers along the escape route, and, sure enough, they found billfolds, watches and rings taken from the hospital.

There was a young man among these three criminals who was married and had two little boys. I talked to the young prisoner—I'll call him," Bill"— and encouraged him to straighten out his life for the sake of his wife and children. I supposed it went in one ear and out the other, for Bill showed no emotion as I talked to him. I never dreamed I would have much impact on his life; however, many years later I met Bill again. By that time, I had retired from the F.B.I. and was working with the Fellow-

Don Lash F.B.I Agent

ship of Christian Athletes in Indiana. One evening Margaret received a call from a man who wanted to talk to me. This was not uncommon since I was working with Christian people. I was not home at the time, but was working about two hours away in rural Indiana on a camp that my family was building So Margaret gave the man directions to the camp and set up an appointment for me to meet him at the nearest neighbor's house at a certain time the next day. After she'd taken his name and hung up the phone, she realized it was Bill...the man I had talked to about changing his life! Margaret panicked for she knew that he might be planning revenge for sending him to prison. She called the neighbor, Mrs. McFadden, at who's house I was to have the appointment. Since there were no phones at the camp, Margaret asked her to go back to the camp, find me, and get in touch with her immediately. Using Mrs. McFadden's phone, I called Margaret right away and she filled me in on the arranged meeting with Bill. When I told Mrs. McFadden our situation, she said, "Don't worry, Don! You stay away from the house and look over the situation. I'll meet him at my front door. If you decide to talk to him, you sit with him out in the yard and I'll be just inside the door with my shot gun!" (Mrs. McFadden was one tough farm lady!) So we followed her plan. As she met Bill at the front door, I sized up the situation and decided that he did not look dangerous. I then came ambling up to the house and we met. Sure enough, it was Bill, the man that I had talked to in Louisville before he went to prison. Bill told me that I was one of the few police officers who had taken the time to help him, and he wanted to thank me for it. He said that he had straightened out his life, but now he had a son who was getting into trouble. Bill asked me to talk to his son and try to help him. I did talk to his son (who had accompanied him) and they left. Mrs. McFadden and I breathed a sigh of relief and laughed about our fear of the situation. Here was a little country woman, a former F.B.I. Agent, and my wife involved in something that had happened years before while I was in the F.B.I.— but it ended all right.

Detroit, Michigan

My next assigned office after Louisville was Detroit. Margaret and the boys stayed at her parent's house until I could find a house in Detroit, because housing was very difficult to acquire during the war. Detroit was a large city with many problems, especially race relations. I arrived in Detroit by train. When I got into a cab to go to the office, the cab windows were broken, and I asked the driver, "What happened?" He told me they were having a race riot and that the National Guard had been called in to patrol the streets! It worked out all right for I was able to find a house and we lived there for one winter. We had lots of sickness that winter with the boys, but when I went to Washington in the spring for in-service training, I asked for a transfer to the southwest. When I got back to my office in Detroit, a transfer to Dallas was waiting for me.

Dallas And Abilene, Texas

At Dallas I was assigned to Abilene as a Resident Agent. New challenges awaited our family there as housing was almost impossible to find in this small Texas town overcrowded by two neighboring military bases. We ended up having to stay with our two small sons in a motel for several weeks and eating all our meals out until we found a home to buy.

Much of my work in Abilene involved the F.B.I.'s jurisdiction over prisoners of war. The government decided the best place to take those prisoners was out to west Texas. Our Agents had the job of rounding up prisoners who had escaped from the stockade. The escapees had no idea how far away from Germany they were, and so they would start walking down the road through the desert. It wasn't long until the chiggers, mosquitoes and heat made them realize it was better back at the camp, and sooner or later, they would find their way back. Our job was easy on these cases for the inmates usually came back on their own. In fact, most of the jobs we had in Abilene were relatively easy ones.

On one occasion, I had gone to Washington for in-service training. I always rode the trains for these long trips. On this particular run, there were no seats available, so I had either to stand or sit on my suitcase all the way from Washington to Dallas. Arriving in Dallas exhausted, I was anxious to get home to Abilene as I climbed into my car and started out on the 180 mile trip home. I was fighting to stay awake when all at once I realized I was off the road and into the ditch! I got out and surveyed the situation. It was very dark and no one was around. I saw that I could get the car back on the road (which I did), and continued on my way home. The Lord took care of me that night, for it was a lonely stretch of highway out in west Texas. I would have been in real trouble if the car had been wrecked or I had been injured. I'm sure that God heard the prayers of Margaret and the boys that night for my safe return.

A memorable case I had in Abilene was one of a runaway girl. The F.B.I. always investigated white slave cases. Since there were so many soldiers around Abilene, prostitutes were plentiful, and it was our job to flush them out and arrest them. One day I went to the jail to interview some of them when I saw a pretty little girl who did not look like she belonged there. As I questioned her, she told me she was 18 years old and from Cleveland, Ohio. She didn't look like she was 18, and her story didn't ring true to me either. After leaving the jail, I headed straight to the police station to check the "missing persons" file. In the file, I found her picture and learned that she was a runaway from a nearby town. When I confronted her with the picture, she admitted she had run away from home because she hated her stepmother. She had managed to get a job at a local cafe, but was paid with a bad check. Alone and without money, she was befriended by some girls whom she thought were wiser than herself. It turned out the "wiser girls" were prostitutes. About that time, all of the girls were picked up by the police and this young runaway was thrown in jail along with the others. We called the sheriff in her home town, and he notified her distraught father. She had been gone 34 days, but she learned that "the man with the badge" was her friend. We got to her in time to prevent her from becoming "one of the girls".

Birmingham, Alabama

My next assignment was Birmingham, and, once again I went on ahead to find a house. Margaret stayed there with our sons to sell the house and organize our furniture for the move to Birmingham. She also had to travel by train, and it was a problem to get the movers and train reservations to come together at the same time. I think she had to stay at a neighbor's house one or two nights after the furniture had gone. In Birmingham we again faced the housing problem, but we finally took a house that was furnished, worked our furniture in with what was already there, and stored the rest of ours in the garage. At least we were not living in a hotel, and we had a home again.

We were living in Birmingham when the atom bomb was dropped on Japan. However, just a few months after settling in, I was transferred to Huntsville, Alabama as a Resident Agent. I would return to Birmingham to dictate my cases, and it was one of these trips that I shall never forget. I had finished part of my dictation and was going to finish the rest of it and start for home the next day. That morning I got on the elevator on the seventh floor of my hotel, when all at once the cable broke sending the elevator to the basement! There was a big spring on the bottom that kept us from crashing, but it also kept us jiggling around awhile. No one was seriously hurt, but one woman fainted. I then went to the office, finished my dictation, got in my car and started home. I was traveling fairly fast when I suddenly came upon a place where they were putting in a bridge. The road was very rough, and I had to slow down to about 15 miles per hour. As I slowed the car down, my steering gear broke, and I went down into the ditch. Uninjured, I called my office and they sent a tow truck to pull me out. By the time the tow truck arrived, it was dark and raining. I was standing out in the road to flag them down when I realized they did not see me. I had to jump into the ditch to keep from getting hit by the truck! Finally I got home about ten o'clock and told Margaret about everything that had happened to me that day. Three times I could have been killed, but God had protected me. She said," Let's get to bed before something else happens!", and we did!

Indianapolis And Lafayette, Indiana

While we were in Huntsville, I received word that the Bureau was looking for a firearms expert to conduct police training schools throughout the country. Since I was an expert marksman, I applied for and received this appointment, and we were sent to Indianapolis. From there I was again transferred as a Resident Agent to Lafayette, Indiana. We were happy to be back in Indiana with family and friends. I traveled all over the west and Midwest conducting police schools. After a few years, I was brought back into the Indianapolis office, because it was closer for me to take planes to my assignments. Indianapolis also afforded me an opportunity to do more police work.

For several years our boys kept asking for a baby sister. While we were moving so much and housing was difficult, we ignored their request for a baby. After the war ended and we were back in Indiana, we considered the situation, but told the boys, "Servicemen have priorities on babies just as they have priorities on other items we'd like to buy!" This seemed to satisfy them. But, after we moved to Indianapolis and had bought a larger house, we "ordered" a little girl. She came in August, and the boys were really happy. We named her Marguerite Sue. She brought us great joy, and we loved her very much. The boys loved her also and, though they teased her as boys always do, she soon learned to hold her own with them.

I was in Indianapolis when I became eligible for retirement from the F.B.I. There were many things that I longed to do, and so, after twenty one years with the Bureau, I took my retirement.

Camp Wapello

I had always dreamed that some day I would start a camp for young people. I expected to locate it in the hills of Brown County, Indiana where boys could run, climb hills and enjoy nature. However, one day at a family reunion of Margaret's family, I learned of a sixty acre plot of ground that had belonged to Margaret's great-grandfather in Parke County. It was rough land with hills and springs of cool water. Margaret's grandfather had raised mules on the land for there was grass, water and hills on which they could roam. After his death, it lay unused and became a liability to the heirs since they had to pay taxes on it. The heirs offered it to me for $1,000.00 cash. The price was reasonable, but I did not have that amount of money. I was anxious to buy it, however, and so I borrowed on my life insurance: a risky thing to do as I was still dodging bullets in the F.B.I. at that time. The boys gave me their savings from their paper routes and together with the savings that we had, we managed to buy "Wapello", as the land was called. Local residents had called the land "Wapello" after the chief of the Fox Indian tribe who had settled there years before the white man came.

I now owned the land but wondered, "How can we make a camp out of it?" The Lord answered me by showing me that if I planted young pine

Lash Family cabin at Wapello.

trees, they could be harvested in about seven years as Christmas trees. He also showed me large trees that could be cut and sawed into lumber for buildings. He inspired me to harness the cool canyon springs for water, haul rocks up from those same canyons to build chimneys and porches, and dig gravel from a pit on the land for roads. The entire family went to work on this project. We spent every cent we could save from my Bureau salary to buy seedlings for Christmas trees. I cut down trees for lumber and had them sawed to build a cabin in which to live when we came down to work. We found water and were able to put in a well. This well proved to be a gift from God. The boys, by now around 12 to 14 years old, had been carrying water up from a spring which was down at the bottom of a steep hill. Water was a very precious commodity at Wapello, and not a drop was ever wasted. A local man water-witched the property and promised there was water available. The boys and I set out to dig our much-needed well by hand. We had gone down about ten feet and, as the walls got higher, we feared the whole thing would cave in on us. We were ready to give up when, sure enough, a small trickle of water began seeping into the hole. God had answered our prayers and shown that water really was down there. There was joy, joy, joy at Wapello that day for water! We still had no electricity, but at least we could pump water and that was easier than carrying it up the hill from the spring! I bought an old tractor and a trailer, and the boys and I proceeded to haul gravel to spread on the road which, up until that time, had been mud paths used by the farmers. We also hauled rocks from the canyon to build a chimney and a foundation for a porch for our cabin. With help from local builders, we built a one room cabin. It was put together from what the land had provided and what I could buy at sales for windows and doors. We even tore down an abandoned BBQ pit in Indianapolis to get some big windows and doors. We were certain we could clean the lettering off the windows, but the words "BBQ" and a picture of a pig always showed through...the smoke from the restaurant having etched the glass. We didn't care! The Lord had provided us with what we needed!

    We loved the land so much that we often brought our high school Sunday School classes from our church in Indianapolis down to Wapello to share in the fun. We would have 30 to 35 young people in our class on Sunday morning but when we invited them for a picnic at Wapello, we would have 90 to 95 young people show up for a day of fun, food and worship.

    The popularity of Camp Wapello began to grow among our friends and church family at Irvington Methodist in Indianapolis. A church friend of ours, Harvey Petty, even presented us with a copy of our camp prayer that he had prepared for us in calligraphy.

    By this time, we had increased our acreage to 150 acres. We now had a large field which was originally the camping ground of the Fox Indians. The boys found many arrowheads and other artifacts left by the Indians.

> **Camp Wapello Prayer**
>
> *Our heavenly Father, creator of all that is nature, we humbly come to you in the midst of nature's splendor to thank you that, as Americans, we are free to worship as we please, work as we please, and move about as we please. To enjoy all that is nature: Its hills, its canyons, its lakes, its streams and the living things that dwell therein. We pray unto you that some day the world may be at peace and all men be free to enjoy nature's abundance. We ask you, in the name of the lord Jesus Christ, that we be guided so that we can protect this priceless heritage which we at Wapello are privileged to enjoy.*
>
> *Amen*

This was a big thrill for all of us. This land gave us access to Sugar Creek and we could go canoeing. Later we built a lake which we stocked with fish for I loved to fish. We sectioned off a part of it for swimming and my now teenage boys and I were life guards for our swimmers.

Next we proceeded to build our largest building which would be our camp lodge. It was here that we had our worship services, our dining room, and our kitchen. All of our funding for the camp was made possible by the sale of our Christmas trees that we had planted in the beginning and which we sold in Indianapolis. A very kind gentleman, Joe Guidone, had a grocery on a busy corner at 10th Street and Arlington in Indianapolis. He wanted to help me with the camp and he allowed us to sell our Christmas trees on the corner of his lot. Selling trees was a big undertaking. The boys and I would cut the trees, haul them in a rented semi to our back yard for storage in Indianapolis. From there I would take them by small trailer loads to the Christmas tree lot. We put up an Indian teepee and sold our "Wapello Christmas Trees". It was hard work, but we enjoyed it because we were helping people enjoy their Christmas as we made money to help build the camp. I would take my vacation time from the F.B.I. for this Christmas tree project. Mr. Hoover knew of my plans to build a camp for young people and even offered to help me financially, but I refused, saying we could do it ourselves. I knew God was helping me and that was all the help I needed.

After the lodge was built, I cut down more trees and we built some sturdy cabins for our young campers. The cabins were rough, but the boys liked to sleep out in the woods and pretend they were fearless men. Our rustic camp was what appealed to young boys. Our own sons added to the "bravery" by telling Indian stories and taking the campers on "snipe hunting" trips at night. The campers also liked canoe trips down

Lash Family selling Christmas trees
(l. to r.) Russell, Don, Marguerite, Margaret & David

Sugar Creek and swimming in the lake. It was an ideal place for young boys, and some of them came back year after year to Camp Wapello.

With all five of our family working together, we began our camp. We enjoyed having young campers but we all worked very hard to make it happen. I directed things, Margaret was the cook, dishwasher, nurse and in charge of morning devotions. The boys and our daughter were in charge of the music, hikes, canoe trips and swimming. With all of us doing our best, we carried on for four summers. Our campers were all good boys whose parents had known me through athletics, F.B.I., or church work and wanted their sons to be under my influence. However, after four years, our boys were out of college. Russ went into the Army and Dave was teaching music in public schools. That left three of us to do the job with the help of two high school counselors. Since we were only charging $50.00 per week per camper, we could not afford to hire help, operate the camp, feed the campers, and pay the bills.

We allowed other groups to enjoy the camp. One particular group was the Ridgefarm (Illinois) Friends Church who came each Labor Day weekend and brought their families and their food. We felt as if they were part of our family, because they came year after year and we watched their children grow. Some other church groups came for a week at a time. But Ridgefarm Friends were especially fond of Wapello and had many happy times there as you can tell by the poem on the opposite page, which was composed anonymously by one of their members the first year the group was unable to return for a long weekend retreat.

One week we had a high school band come down for their band camp. This was quite an experience for there were ninety of them, and we were really stretched to house and feed them. To add to all this excitement, their cooks failed to show up for duty! Fortunately, with the help of two band member's mothers and two friendly neighbors from the local community, we managed to feed them, planning one meal at a time all week long. It certainly was with God's help for we could never have done it alone.

God had provided me with Wapello, this secluded spot far away from people and traffic, where I could be alone with Him. I would sometimes slip off to the camp just to be alone with God when things didn't go the way I thought they should at the Bureau. It was comforting to know I could drive out to Wapello and talk things over with God. Not surprisingly, He always understood!

Someone gave me this poem which seemed to express my feeling for Wapello:

> There's a path that leads
> through the woodland,
> a path I love to trod...
> to get away from this wild world's rush
> and be alone with God."

Farewell To Wapello – A Camper's Lament

It just didn't seem like Labor Day Weekend, did it? We didn't see Harriet with a shopping list in her hand, busy buying the necessities for forty people (more or less) for three days. No packing and repacking of food and supplies. No cleaning up and applying Lysol in the showers. No making chili for Friday night, applying the "remains" to the Saturday night hot dog!

How can a person count up the joys and pleasures of being with the Lash's at Camp Wapello? Let's give it a try .... remember when Clay and Olive Miller did our cooking? Wasn't that the best food you ever ate? Fried chicken — hmmm good!

Wally Deck, the year he went "all out" in softball, sacrificing the seat of his pants! Canoeing down Sugar Creek, quietly skimming along, catching the beauty of nature on either side, and having fish jump into the canoe.

Those wild, wet water tournaments reigning King of the Mountain on a tractor tire! Freezing at 42 degrees but loving every minute of it. Going downhill on "Jacob's Ladder" and wondering whether you'd ever make it to the top again. Taking the "tour" down the canyon with Don as our guide. The fishermen eating their "catch" for Sunday breakfast. That Neal Young showed them all how to catch 'em big. Pancakes and sausage ... do you remember how many pancakes that Steve Majors could put away?

Candlelight service- - the awesome quiet as each said, "You are the light of the world!" The candles floating out on the lake...the meaning of it all.

Keith Williams growing in knowledge after sleeping(???) in the boy's cabin. He really believed those stories! Carol Biederman finding a mouse in her bed! The "wolves" scratching at the walls of the girl's cabin. Bill McCartney falling overboard in all his fishing finery. Dale Romoser going off the pulley and into the lake...clothes and all!! Singing Moffats Lord's Prayer together after meeting with Eugene Coffin. Making stuffed animals and wind chimes. Going down to the clay pit. How about that, Walter whistling in the "john"? Snipe hunting with that tricky Marguerite? Those mornings in September when I stepped out of my cabin down in "Bear Hollow", the bushes shining with the "diamonds" left by the sun on spider webs and the air crisp and cool- it made me feel like Adam in the Garden of Eden... and required to share the glory with nobody but God. So I say, "Farewell, Wapello!", and store those happy memories in the Bank of the Past.

Methodist Family Of The Year

In 1961 our family was chosen as "Methodist Family of the Year" for the Indianapolis District of the Methodist Church. We were selected because of the way we projected Christ in our church youth work, our service to the community, and the example I set through athletics for young people. We represented our District in Chicago at the national convention, which was quite an honor for all of us.

In selecting our family for this honor, our church, Irvington Methodist, noted the following in their monthly newsletter, *The Spire*, in April, 1961:

"Donald and Margaret Lash have three children, Russell, 22; David, 20 and Marguerite, 11. In selecting them for this honor you have chosen well. "Don" is a member of The official board at our church, has taught Sunday School for twenty years in the high school department and has served as chairman of our Vocation Committee. He has been a Special Agent for the F.B.I. for twenty years. He is best remembered by many, however, for his outstanding record in athletics. Because of his record and his Christian spirit, he served as a member of the Advisory Committee of the State and National Fellowship of Christian Athletes. For the last twenty nine years he has volunteered himself for a continuous series of tests in the I.U. Physiology Laboratory. He is a volunteer instructor in first aid and swimming for the American Red Cross and for the Y.M.C.A. Youth groups and service clubs have called upon him as a public speaker for twenty five years where he stresses Christian living and physical fitness. He entertains hundreds of young people at his cabin near Turkey Run State Park, where he plans to open a family-sponsored youth camp in the near future emphasizing Christian living through artistic expression and athletics."

Fellowship Of Christian Athletes

One day, while I was still with the F.B.I., a Presbyterian minister in Indianapolis, named Roe Johnston, introduced me to the Fellowship of Christian Athletes (F.C.A.). This was an organization founded to influence young athletes to Christianity through the testimony of big name athletes. F.C.A. had some outstanding present day and former athletes who were Christians and were willing to give their time to attend conferences throughout the United States witnessing to youth. I was interested in this organization for I felt it important to teach young people about Christ. After retiring from the F.B.I., I joined this organization and became their first Regional Director. It was my privilege to represent F.C.A. in a five-state area, including Illinois, Indiana, Ohio, Wisconsin and Michigan. I would go to colleges and high schools setting up "Huddle Groups" among their athletes. I traveled quite a bit and gave hundreds of speeches to schools, service clubs and churches. I then would attend F.C.A's National Conferences which were held during the summer months at Y.M.C.A. facilities at Estes Park Colorado, North Carolina, Wisconsin, and New York. This was a great experience for me, as well as for my family. In it's early days, F.C.A. was primarily an all-male organization, and to hear 600 male voices singing "How Great Thou Art" was a thrill that brought tears to my eyes. These conferences were unforgettable to all of us, and afforded us the opportunity to hear some truly outstanding speakers who were also Christian athletes.

While I was a Regional Director for the F.C.A., we still enjoyed Wapello as a family. But the stresses of traveling with the organization made it harder for me to maintain the camp and spend time with my family. Still, I felt Wapello should be enjoyed by youth of all ages.

One snowy winter day I was walking through the camp and enjoying the hills and the quietness of the snow when suddenly in front of me on the snow were two large drops of blood. There were no animal tracks, no birds overhead and no explanation for them. This seemed to me to be a sign from God that I should give up the camp or it would be my death. I studied the situation and prayed about it for many days. Finally I decided I should give up my beloved Wapello. I offered to sell it to the F.C.A. for a conference site where they could hold their summer conferences. They were willing to buy the property if I could raise the money to purchase it. I agreed to find the funding, and went to John Lynn of the Lilly Endowment. Mr. Lynn agreed to give me the money so that F.C.A. could buy the camp.

Thus, I sold my beloved Wapello. It represented fifteen years of hard work on the part of all five of us. Moreover, it represented all of our savings for fifteen years. I felt God had given the land to me to develop and to share with others. I had accomplished this, and now the F.C.A. could develop it further and share it with thousands more.

Over the years, the Fellowship has been given a great deal of money to develop the camp in ways I could not do on my own. Thousands of people, both young and old, have come to this beautiful facility in Marshall, Indiana known as the National Resource and Training Center for the Fellowship of Christian Athletes. Here they have come to commune with God, see the beauty of the land, and enjoy the quietness that envelops the spot far away from the restless world.

I always loved to go back to the camp after I sold it, for it was at Wapello that God spoke to me and I felt His presence and direction in developing the camp. I especially loved watching the deer, fishing in the lake, wandering through the canyon to see the layers of coal, shale, and clay, and skipping stones across the small stream early settlers used for their water supply and turning their grist mill. In that same canyon, Fox Indians hunted wild turkeys from the cliffs, and just next to the camp's athletic field, I could walk among the ruins of the last settler's charred cabin. God's creation and American history blended in harmony together on this land. I have traveled around the world and lived in many states, but my heart has always been and will remain at Wapello.

After serving with the F.C.A. for several years, I felt a calling to go in other directions. We still loved beautiful Parke County, Indiana and wanted to remain in the same vicinity as the camp. Margaret and I started a real estate business in nearby Rockville, and we encouraged our son, David, to join us while he finished his doctorate degree at Indiana University. I ran for the office of Trustee of Indiana University and was elected. I served there two years before deciding I could do more for my fellow Hoosiers by serving in the Indiana General Assembly. I resigned from the Trustee position so that there would be no conflict of interest in my decisions as a State Representative.

I was successful in my bid as a State Representative, and served there for ten years. By that time, I was having trouble with my heart and underwent five bypasses. The doctors advised me to give up activities that caused stress. There had been stress on my heart in athletics, in the F.B.I., with the Fellowship and in politics.

Thus I resigned from these activities and assisted Margaret and David in the real estate business. I enjoyed this line of work, because I felt our customers needed honest professionals helping them with their real estate problems. Margaret and I gained a great deal of experience buying and renting houses while in the F.B.I., and we had moved thirteen times in our married life. We purchased an older building in Rockville (what had once served as the blacksmith shop), renovating it while preserving it's historical heritage, and established Lash Realtors.

Reflections On
The Indiana General Assembly

My ten years in the Indiana General Assembly were stressful, but interesting. I have recorded my thoughts about the responsibilities of public officials and presented them to my fellow representatives when I retired from that office. That speech is presented below:

I feel most fortunate in having served my District for the past decade here in the Indiana General Assembly. Actually, I feel that anyone who serves in the General Assembly has an awesome responsibility to his people simply because he is making the very laws under which we live and work every day of our lives.

I feel that legislators should be working for the good of the people and should contribute to society. The compensation should be small compared to other professions. Full time, well-paid government employees at the expense of the taxpayer, is not the spirit in which this government was born. I feel that the legislator's gift should come from the heart, with a willingness to sacrifice and work hard for the good of the entire community ... not for his personal gain. I cannot help but feel the public should be made aware of the shortcomings of legislators who fail to meet these standards. It is the public's responsibility to work to elect good people to represent them, not vote for the party nor even the immediate cause at hand, but for the good of the state and district.

At this time, I really don't know of a better system of government, and yet I certainly am not satisfied with the present system. I have seen many legislators lose sight of what the true spirit of making laws should be when they are put to the test. For example, I have seen lobbyists bring pressure on members of the General Assembly, either to make a law or to change a law in favor of the lobbyists or a group which they represent. Many politicians will try to make you believe that the large corporations are the only ones who are guilty of unethical lobbying, but this is far from the truth. Take for example a person who works for a union. There are people in unions who lobby to enhance their departments just for the sake of increasing it. Again, a labor organization will often spend millions of dollars to aid their memberships through their lobbying efforts. On the day that a bill is being considered, the unions will bus large numbers of their members to the State House to pressure each legislator and even threaten him.

I have no quarrel with the individual who, after voting for his legislator, contacts that legislator and expresses his thoughts. I always welcomed those letters and calls. But it does not seem right to me for an organization, through influence, gifts, and threats to intimidate and practically force a legislator to vote for their cause. I do not have the answer to lobbying, but I have seen the effects of what I call improper lobbying in the Legislature. Our government is made up of the Executive, Judicial, and the Legislative branches. I have seen all three branches try to supersede each other, and which, again, is not what our forefathers had in mind. I feel that the Legislative branch of the government is the one which should make the laws. Today the courts have far expanded on their powers: they not only interpret the laws, but actually make the laws. And the same might be said from the President on down. These branches often try to expand their office through coercion of the other two offices. I cannot help but feel that this is going to become a greater problem unless each branch is held within its confines.

I have always believed in freedom of the press, but, during my tenure in office, I have seen some members of the press take advantage of this freedom. They have printed material as the truth when it was not... regardless of the tremendous harm it might do to an individual, a cause, or a political party.

I personally feel that the Legislature should be made up of people who have had a great deal of experience and success in life. It should not be made up of those with little or no experience in the business world or those who have failed at everything else. If some legislators cannot even run their own business, how can they expect to run the affairs of our State?

Perhaps the saddest situation in the General Assembly is the waste of both money and time by the large number of bills prepared every year by the Legislative Council at the request of legislators. Many of the Legislators seem to feel that they are "God's Gift to the Political World", and in order to enhance their position with their constituents, must present many bills. As a result, over a thousand bills are prepared in one year with most of them never even seeing the light of day! Of course, this "presentation" gives some members of the Legislature an opportunity to appear before the rest of us and display their theatrical talents for the benefit of the media and the public with hopes of advancing themselves politically. If these legislators were sincere and would present one good solid bill of their own or if they have other legislation which would help the state and the world, it could be shared with anothers to be presented in the upcoming session. This procedure would save the State of Indiana many dollars and the sessions would be shortened. With better planning, we could give more time to good and necessary legislation.

I have been most fortunate in serving under Governor Otis Bowen. I first knew Dr. Bowen as a fraternity brother at Indiana University, and I have respected him down through the years. He is a man who is honest and has set a good example for others to follow. The leadership in both Houses has been good during my ten years, and, again, I feel most fortunate. There have been times, however, when the social drinking, cocktail parties, dinners and banquets which were put on by the lobbyists went beyond the best interests of the people of our state. Here again, however, I feel that this is the individual responsibility of each legislator. Fortunately most legislators did not fall into this category.

Many of our legislative assistants went far beyond their call of duty in offering help to us in the General Assembly. No doubt the experience that they have received in assisting members of the Legislature will be of great value to them. However, I do feel that it would be a mistake for these young people to seek elective offices without first getting a knowledge of the outside world. I feel that, by working in the business world before they enter politics, they will find out first hand what it takes to make a living and to meet responsibilities.

During the past decade, many people have befriended and helped me, and for that I am grateful. It seems fitting and proper for this portion in my life to come towards the end of a career which has taken me through athletics, 21 years as a Special Agent of the F.B.I., developing and running a boy's camp, and owning a real estate business. All of these chapters of my life are very worthy, but my career has been highlighted by representing my people in the Indiana General Assembly. Now I feel that it is time to close this chapter of my life and get on with the business at hand.

Message delivered upon retirement from the Indiana General Assembly.

To Margaret & Donald Lash
Best wishes
J. Edgar Hoover
3.27.67

Lash Family with J. Hoover at F.B.I. Headquarters. (l.to r.)
Russell E. Lash, Donald R. Lash, Margaret Lash, J. Edgar Hoover,
Elizabeth Lash, Marguerite Lash and David R. Lash.

Retirement

One of the proudest moments of my life was to visit Washington D.C. when both of my sons were F.B.I. Agents. By now my sons were both married and we all visited J. Edgar Hoover, and had our picture taken with him. It is always gratifying to a father when his sons follow in his footsteps and this was a proud moment in my life.

After retiring from the General Assembly, I had more time to help others. I was the first President of the Vermilion County Foundation to raise money for Vermilion County Hospital. I served as President of the Parke County Historical Society which compiled a book of the history of Parke County. I also helped a local group get organized to assist the underprivileged in Parke County with food, clothes and health needs. I now had time to do things I felt were important in meeting the needs of my community. Retirement is, I believe, a time to remain active! I have always ended my speaking engagements by saying, "I want to keep going until I hear my Heavenly Father say,' Well done, My good and faithful servant!'

Auburn, Indiana

Even though I have lived in many places and in many states, I always think of Auburn, Indiana as my home town. I am proud to say I grew up in Auburn! I have fond memories of the local people who influenced my life: my high school coach, Cecil (Zeke) Young; C.C. Cripe, the minister of our church; my teachers; and, the boys that I ran with in athletics. It was here that I remember my parents, and how hard my mother worked to keep food on the table during The Great Depression when work for my father was uncertain. I especially remember how proud of me the townspeople were when I began to make headlines in the papers with my running. But most of all I remember how the people of Auburn went together and put on a fund raiser to raise money for me to go to the Olympics in Berlin, Germany. The townspeople of Auburn provided all the money for my trip, and even bought me a trunk with my initials, D.R.L., printed on it! I can never forget their generosity and hard work so that I could make the trip. I was so proud to represent Auburn, Indiana University, and America in Berlin.

I always kept in contact with Zeke and Violet Young whenever I came back to Indiana. They have both passed on, but they were my most loyal supporters. Now I have learned that the city is going to name a park in my honor and call it the Don Lash Park. I feel very honored to have a park named for me. The people of Auburn, Indiana are very special people to me and I am thankful that I grew up in a small town with so many caring and loving people.

Closing Thoughts

Spiritually, I have always felt that I was a "special" one with God, because everything always seemed to go my way. From the time in my grandfather's upstairs bedroom when I saw the bright, angelic light, many times when I was in grade school, and on up through my career, I felt His presence. There are lots of things I received in life that I didn't deserve: like getting to go to college when I had no money and many other things that have gone my way. I know God has provided. I know it was all planned long before I ever thought about it. God has always been with me and taken care of me. Even now, I know I am dying with cancer and He is with me. I can feel the presence of God almost anytime I think of it. I don't worry about tomorrow for He has said, "He who is first in this world will be last in the next ,and he who is last in this world will be first in the next". Of course I was denied many things and have had my share of trouble, but, on the other hand, I had so many opportunities that I have been able to do a whole lot more with my life than the average person. I feel God has planned my life and I just fit in and followed along. Margaret has been a part of this life and I feel that we will be together always. I will keep going until I hear those words, "Well done My good and faithful servant!" I am glad that I have had the opportunity to serve Him and to witness for Him. Thank You, God!

Don Lash in Olympic suit at Indiana University.

Stories, Letters And Speeches

To know Don Lash was to know a man with several facets to his personality. You have just read the first person account of his life, but to really understand the man, we've included some information and stories about him by others, letters and speeches that give insight into his character, and finally some personal stories by him that provide a hint about his sense of humor. Anyone who knew Don, can testify that he, while quite serious about God, America and the importance of clean living, also had a humorous side. In the section titled, "Cock-'n-Bull Stories", we share some of the best-loved, not-totally-true stories he shared with family and friends.

Tributes
By Margaret Lash

Don left us and went to be with God on September 19, 1994. His last wish was to have his funeral at his beloved Wapello. Larry Medcalfe was the Director of the F.C.A. Camp at the time and he allowed Don's funeral service to be held in the camp chapel. As we drove out the lane to go to the cemetery, there stood a deer looking at us as if to say," Good bye, friend! We'll miss you!"

By Jane Sewell, Ridgefarm Friends Church, Ridgefarm, Illinois

Farewell Dear Friend—To those of us who enjoyed the experience of going to Camp Wapello every Labor Day weekend for six years, knowing Don and Margaret Lash was a special privilege in our lives. Don Lash was a man's man, a family man, a Christian man, a storyteller, a humorist, a camper, a builder, a listener, and a friend.

Going to Wapello was a spiritual, recreational and physical retreat for our families. There seemed to be no "generation gap". We all enjoyed the Lash family.

Now our children have children and Wapello is part of the past. It's memories we cherish. We may not know all the precious seeds planted in the minds and hearts of young lives by Don and Margaret, but we do know some of those seeds have grown and are bearing fruit.

I am the Resurrection and the Life. He who believes me shall never die."

Married Life
By Margaret Lash

On January 27, 1937 I was having to stay on at Indiana University. It was final exam time, I was finished with my finals but because I was a waitress at the girl's dormitory, I had to stay until all of the girls in the dorm were finished with their exams. I was feeling a bit lonesome when a boy that I had been dating and who worked in the girl's dorm asked me for a date that evening. I was glad to have something to do so I said, "Yes." We probably went out for a coke at the "Book Nook" and then went for a walk. I do not remember many details about that part of the evening. There was a full moon and lots of snow on the ground. One of our favorite places to walk was behind the dorm where there were two or three wooden bridges. On one of these bridges we stopped and looked at the beautiful moon and the glistening snow. Then my boyfriend began telling me his life story. He told about his brother and four sisters, his mother and father and even his grandparents. After he told me all of the facts and some of the hardships he had through Depression years and about his sister who was in a hospital, he asked me hesitatingly if I would marry him. I was quite surprised because he was a "big man on the campus" in athletics and could have any girl he desired for a wife! I could hardly believe my ears when I heard myself saying, "Yes!" Then he gave me a little gold shoe on a gold chain which was his Balfour Award shoe with diamonds and rubies. He also gave me his fraternity pin which was jeweled with rubies and pearls and with a "large diamond" in the center. I was so overwhelmed with the necklace, the pin, and my decision to say, "Yes!" I am not sure if my feet ever touched the ground as we walked back to the dorm. Here was a little freshman farm girl from Pendleton at Indiana University promising to marry the famous athlete, Don Lash, who had just returned from the 1936 Olympics. Was this real ... or was I dreaming? We walked back to the dorm, had a good night kiss, and I ran up to my room. My roommate, who just the night before had asked me if I would say, "Yes" to a proposal and I had said, "No", could hardly believe her ears when I told her! I took off my jeweled fraternity pin and my jeweled gold shoe necklace and put them under my pillow. I slept with them under my pillow until we were married on June 18, 1938 in the Little Church Around the Corner in New York City.

Don was always sympathetic to those who were poor and in need of help. This was probably due to the fact that his family was poor as he was growing up, and he could sympathize with them.

One time, on one of his trips to New York, he stopped in to get a sandwich before starting home on the train. There was an old man and his son sitting on the stools next to him. In their conversation, the son was chastising his father mercilessly because he was "down and out" and had no money for food. Don felt so sorry for the older man that he took a $10 bill out of his pocket and dropped it on the floor next to the father. Then Don picked it up and gave it to the old man saying, "Here, you must have dropped this!" Then he walked out leaving the two men at the counter.

Another time he was in a store in downtown Indianapolis doing some checking on one of his cases in the F.B.I. when he noticed a little old lady. She was dressed shabbily and he noticed that her undergarments were falling down around her ankles. She was trying to pull them up. He went to a clerk of the store and gave her some money telling her to get the lady some new undergarments. The last time he saw them, the clerk was helping the lady with some new underwear.

I remember our first Thanksgiving after we were married. Don was a State Policeman and brought home a pay check of $92.00 per month. We were making ends meet but that was about all we were doing. Just before Thanksgiving he arrested a young man who was then sent to jail. It was Don's duty to go out to his parents and tell them what had happened to their son. They lived out in the hill country around Bloomington, Indiana. Their house was dirty, the parents were wearing dirty clothes, and the children were dirty as well. They told him that they would have no Thanksgiving dinner for they had no money. So Don promised that we would bring them their Thanksgiving dinner. When he came home and told me, I was perplexed! Thanksgiving dinner for us was to be meatloaf, because we could not afford turkey or even chicken. However, we scraped together and made 2 meat loaves, pumpkin pie and some other things and drove out to take it to them on Thanksgiving Day. We were both surprised because they were all cleaned up, and the father had even scraped the tobacco juice off the front of the heating stove! I felt sure that they were expecting turkey, but it was not in our budget that year.

Pop Bottles And Change
By Russell Lash

My dad, Don Lash, worked out with some form of physical exercise nearly everyday of his life. Exercise was almost like a religion to him, and I didn't fully appreciate his way of thinking until I was an adult.

When we lived in Lafayette, Indiana, I was six or seven years old, and Dad would want my brother David and me to accompany him to the Purdue University field house. I didn't want to go, because it was boring to watch dad run around the track and look after my younger brother. Mom would chide me into going by saying, "It will hurt his feelings if you don't go!" Now when I look back, I think she just wanted to get rid of two little mischievous boys for a few hours.

One day in the field house, dad came up to us after his work out and said, "Come here boys I want to show you something." Under the field house bleachers from the basketball game the night before was all the litter from the fans: pop bottles, paper cups, empty popcorn boxes, etc. Dad walked up to an empty box and picked up a dime. I'm sure he had spotted the dime earlier, but he sure made it look easy to find the loose change that had slipped out of student's pockets at the basketball game. "Wow!," I thought, "What a gold mine!" The three of us set off looking for loose change under the bleachers. I was so excited that time flew by, and dad had to scold me to go home.

There is a saying that all good things must come to an end, and our "gold mine" came to an end later on when the bleachers collapsed during a basketball game. Many students were seriously hurt. But my childhood "gold mine" days linger in my mind to this day. Dad used this time to encourage David and me in running. After we had finished scavenging for pop bottles and loose change, dad would challenge us to a 100 yard dash, with Dave on the 50 yard line and me on the forty-five. Dad would let us win the first race, but would beat us in the next two. We would even take our bicycles to the track and try to beat dad in the 440 (with a head start, of course).

Dad and I continued running together, and one day, a few years later, we started out together and I finished just ahead of him in the 100 yard dash. For me, beating the great Don Lash was just as exciting as finding the dime under the bleachers!

Later, dad came to all my school track meets, and just his presence at the side of the track would make me feel invincible. I never needed dad's presence more than in the state mile finals at Tech High School in May, 1958. Earlier that year, I had endured back surgery after suffering from back pain so intensely severe I just wanted to die to get relief. The surgery was successful and I recovered, but I was in no condition to defend my win from the year before. I asked dad to stand on the last curve before the final straight away of the finish line. He was a bit perplexed at my request, because he always stood at the 220 mark shouting my time as I ran past. My plan was to run to complete exhaustion and be in the first place when I collapsed at dad's feet on the curve. Since "old man pain" and I were such good friends by now, and I had no fear of death, I planned to end it all right there.

I didn't die that day, but I did win the race. I'll never forget looking up at dad after the race in a semi-conscious state and seeing his blue F.B.I. suit completely imbrued in sweat: he looked as exhausted as I did!

Years later after that fateful day in May at the state finals, I realized I had won the race because of my dad, Don Lash. Although I was unaware of it at the time, he ran every step with me and carried me from his position on the curve, down the straight away, and across the finish line in front of all the contenders.

The Fishing Trip
By Jean Lash

My brother, Don Lash, enjoyed fishing all of his life, but I remember one particular fishing trip when I was about ten or twelve years old that I really ruined for him. Don was several years older than me and had come home to take my dad, Brandon, and me fishing at a local lake near Auburn. Mother had packed us a picnic lunch, and we started out early for a day at the lake. However, not long after we baited our hooks and tossed our lines in the water, I got hungry and decided I'd go back to the car and get one of the sandwiches. Dad had locked the car and taken the keys, and I knew I didn't dare interrupt the men while they were fishing. Leaning my fishing pole against the car, I stood on the running board of the car, stretched in through a slightly opened window, and unlocked the door. Satisfied with myself, I snatched a sandwich and plunked down beside the car to eat it while the men fished. But just as quickly as I sat down, I stood up and screamed! I had sat down on my own fishing hook from the pole I'd leaned up against the car! I had hooked myself right where I sat down!

When I screamed, the men came running! Dad couldn't extract the hook, so they had to call off the fishing trip to take me to the doctor! Of course, I couldn't sit down, and so I stood on the car's running board all the way to the doctor's office. When we got there, Dad tried to console me while the doctor removed the hook. He told me later he could hardly bear the sight of me in such pain, and could have taken it better if my mother had been the one with the hook in her! Don was just plain mad at me for ruining his fishing trip, and he said that I deserved the pain for trying to steal one of the sandwiches!

Letters, Memos, News Articles, And Speeches

To: Tom J. Miller, Bloomington, IN
From: Donald R. Lash

Thank you for your letter of November 14 in regards to some of the stories of former athletes which appear in the football and basketball programs.

Since I am not writing this story, it is rather difficult for an amateur like myself to say what you would like to know; therefore, I am sending to you what I call a "Fact Sheet", a copy of an article which appeared in *Sports Illustrated* on December 12, 1988, and a copy of a story in the Clinton, Indiana newspaper, "The Clintonian".

The reason I went to IU was because of Coach E.C. Hayes, who not only was a great coach, but a great teacher and a molder of boys into men. I quote from the *Sports Illustrated* story, "(Don Lash) was probably the first great American distance runner." This, of course, is the world's oldest sport and (I believe my success) was all because of Coach Billy Hayes. In addition, I held American records in the two, three, four and five mile runs, plus the 5,000 and 10,000 meter runs. I received the L.G. Balfour Awards in 1935-36-37, the Jake Gimbel Award while at IU, and the Z.G. Clevenger Award in 1974.

I will be attending the Hall of Fame Banquet this coming Friday evening and will be staying overnight at the IU Memorial Union. If you have questions that you would like to ask, please do not hesitate to give me a call or we could meet early Saturday morning.

> Thank you for your kindness...
> DRL

* * *

TO: Jack Kavanagh, N. Kingstown, R.I.
FROM: Donald R. Lash
DATE: February, 1987

Thank you for your letter of February 2, 1987 making inquiry about my recollections of the 1936 Olympics in Berlin, Germany and Tarzan Brown. I will do my best to refresh my memory and to answer some of your questions concerning Tarzan Brown.

As I recall, he had come from an underprivileged family much like myself. It is true that I gained ten pounds on the trip over to Berlin, and I recall that Tarzan also gained weight. We traveled on the Manhattan of the U.S. Lines, and the food was excellent! On the surface, it would look like we gorged ourselves on food; however, in my case, I had been training hard and running the mile and two-mile races in collegiate competition. I continued to eat my normal amount, but was unable to train on the voyage without getting shin splints on a rolling boat. In the Olympics, I jumped from the mile and two-mile races to the 5,000 and 10,000 meter races, which were difficult for me to do. Another factor that worked to my disadvantage was that my races were scheduled immediately after we landed, and I did not have time to train after getting off the boat. The record will speak for itself, but I recall that I finished eighth in the finals in one of my races. We were unable to exercise and if we had still eaten the same amount of food, we still would have gained approximately the same weight because of our lack of exercise.

Both Tarzan and myself did our best, especially since this was one of the hottest summers in Berlin that was ever recorded. As I said before, it was difficult for me to jump from the mile and two mile races to the 5,000 and 10,000 meters.

After the 1936 Olympics, I set a world record in the two-mile run in the Boston Garden in 1937, and was able to win seven consecutive National Championships in Cross Country. This record stands today. I also won the Sullivan Award in 1938. I think we must also realize that both Tarzan and myself expanded more energy in just one distance than Jesse did in all three of his races. This is not to belittle Jesse, because he was one of the finest sprinters of his day, even though now all of his records have been broken.

I feel that the acid test of all sports is, "Does it make us a better person and make us want to contribute to society?" I think all writers of ancient history of sports should take a second look at this as they judge athletes. I know very little about Tarzan Brown's life after 1936. I was able to follow Jesse, because I was in the F. B. I. and knew the agents in the territory were Jesse lived. I also followed some others who were in the 1936 Olympics.

When I was young, my ambition was to help others and I will give you a short resume of what happened to me after my competition:

I served 21 years in the F. B. 1. as a Special Agent and am on retirement from the government at this time. After retiring from the Bureau, I started a non-profit camp for youth in the summertime. I became the first Regional Director in the United States for the Fellowship of Christian Athletes. The Fellowship now has the camp which is now their National Resource and Training Center. I served in the Indiana Legislature for ten years where I was never defeated in an election. My wife and I started the Don Lash Realtors Company, and I have now turned that over to my son. I have received many service awards for community service, such as the American Institute for Public Service Jefferson Award. I have served on hospital boards and local community boards.

I apologize that I have not done more. I feel someone should research how much good, if any, athletic participation does for a young person in preparing him or her for a life of service to the world.

Thank you for your letter, and if I can be of further service in any way, please do not hesitate to call upon me.

DRL

✻ ✻ ✻

TO: Evan Bayh, Governor of Indiana
FROM: Donald R. Lash
DATE: February 21, 1989

As a retired F.B.I. Agent, as a retired State Representative, and as an active Christian all my life, I am very much opposed to gambling of any kind in Indiana.

It is true that many voters voted for gambling in November for the simple reason that they thought that the gambling proceeds would take the place of their state taxes. They, of course, have been mislead; however, I am sure that they will expect a tax refund if the gambling bill passes.

A study of the states that have gambling reflects that these are the very states that have the most financial troubles; moreover, the same study shows that most people who gamble are the very ones who pay the least amount of taxes, and many are on public welfare.

Please consider these facts and please veto any legislation on gambling passed by the Indiana House of Representatives and the Senate.

Respectfully yours,
DRL
CC: *The Indianapolis Star*

* * *

TO: Mr. Fred D. Cavinder, Editor, *Indianapolis Star* Magazine
FROM: Donald R. Lash

Enclosed is my article on the Sullivan Award. Also enclosed are some pictures. I would appreciate their return upon your use of them. If you have any questions, please do not hesitate to call me at my home in Rockville, Indiana. Also enclosed is a background information sheet. You have my permission to delete or improve the story as you may see fit.

(Biographical sketch was included along with the following comments:)

I could not believe what I had just heard while watching television recently! A doctor was being interviewed about athletes and the use of drugs. He stated that he saw nothing wrong with the use of drugs in the upcoming Olympics and that the United States had to win at all costs!

In my opinion, this doctor had missed the very purpose of athletics. Athletics should never be used as an end in itself but as a means to better one's life. Millions of young people, including myself, learned through athletics that self discipline paid off and that it was through discipline and not drugs that one can achieve one's goals.

To me, the James E. Sullivan Award is the highest honor that an amateur athlete can receive. The recipient has competed with honor and distinction. He or she has not competed for money, but for the love of the sport, as well as the institution and the people that s/he represented.

The true greatness of an athlete cannot be measured in awards or honors, but in how much that athlete contributes to society and what s/he may do with his or her life. I have met or followed nearly all of the Sullivan Award winners since Bobby Jones, and most all of have contributed much to our society.

This is one of the great benefits of athletics. It keeps an athlete with heart and character in the race of life, long after his athletic days are over. He simply does not give up. He masters himself ... he is not a quitter.

For me, the James E. Sullivan Award did not come easy. Once you have become a champion, all of the other athletes are out to defeat you. On many occasions, I started a race and felt that I could never finish the race, let alone win. I seemed to be tired: tired from the long train ride from Indiana to New York or Boston, tired from school and workouts, and even tired from the race the weekend before. For example, when the call came for the mile run, my coach and everyone I held dear expected great things from me in the race. I felt that I could not let them down so at least I would start the race. I secretly would tell myself, "I can at least run the first quarter and stay with the pack, I may be forced to drop out later." By the time I had finished the first quarter, I felt that perhaps I could stay until the end of the half mile and that would look even better! At the end of the half mile, I felt that I could run another quarter, and when I had run the third quarter, I would realize that I had only one quarter more to go and I would give it all I had and finish the race. The end result was, if I didn't win, at least I was able to conquer myself! I had run the race and had the satisfaction of knowing that I had done a job and had given it all I had.

Strange as it may sound, every time that God has granted me a privilege, He has extracted from me a responsibility. Those who have received the Sullivan Award indeed have a responsibility in setting an example for themselves and others to follow. This athlete has been selected by sports writers and former winners as the most outstanding amateur athlete in the United States which includes all sports.

I personally have benefited much from my athletic background during the past fifty years: first as a Special Agent of the F. B. I. and even to the present day. When I reached 51 years of age, I had developed angina which was caused by calcium in my blood vessels near the heart. At that time, surgery had not been developed and the attending physician advised me that my larger vessels could no longer carry blood to and from my heart. But due to my athletic background, the small vessels were enlarged and they could possibly carry enough blood to keep me going for a few more years. The fact that I was a non-smoker, which had carried over from my athletic days, had saved my life to that point. Twenty years later when the smaller vessels were getting blocked, I had by-pass surgery which is now giving my heart sufficient blood. I now look forward to life as much as the day when I received the Sullivan Award.

I am proud to be a Hoosier, an American, and the recipient of the Sullivan Award. I firmly believe that the lives of the athletes speak for the award itself. Indianapolis is to be congratulated on being the Amateur Sports Center of the United States. There is no doubt in my mind that millions of young people have and will use amateur sports as a means to help achieve higher goals in their lives. I have no fear for the future as long as the spirit and the integrity of the Sullivan Award is applied in the lives of our young people.

* * *

TO: Stephen L. Harris, Westport, CT
FROM: Donald R. Lash
DATE: January 2, 1992

Thank you for your letter of December 1, 1991 in which you asked for remembrances of the 1936 Olympics. Having served as a Special Agent of the F. B. I., I know your problem in investigating this past history, especially since it happened over 50 years ago.

I do remember that Helen Hayes and her husband and the entire Olympic Committee were on board the *Manhattan* of the U.S. Lines. There were many rumors and the only thing I can report are rumors and nothing else. My information is strictly second-hand information. I might point out also that I knew every member of the Olympic Committee, and I am positive that Glen Morris had absolutely nothing to do with their decision concerning Eleanor Holm Jarrett. At that time he had not won the decathlon and was just like all other members of the Olympic team.

The rumor concerning Eleanor was that when we arrived at LaHarve France, Eleanor was in her state room, and she supposedly threw a bottle at a policeman outside on the dock. When several members of the Olympic Committee approached her in her state room about this matter, she was supposed to have been disrobed and somewhat intoxicated. They dismissed her from the team at that time. I saw her later and she was in tears.

One thing we should keep in mind, however, is that the morals and standards of conduct of that time were quite different from what they are today for members of the Olympic team. For example, rumor has it that the Olympic Committee is considering allowing Magic Johnson to be a member of the upcoming Olympic team. He never would have made it in 1936. First, he is a professional player, and, second, I understand that he has admitted having intercourse out of wedlock.

I was never involved in Olympia and know nothing further concerning Glen Morris.

I wish you success in your upcoming book on the Olympic Decathlon.

                                      Sincerely,
                                      DRL

✲ ✲ ✲

TO: Mr. Frank Borns, Manager, Indianapolis, IN Union Station Restoration
FROM: Donald R. Lash

After hearing your request for "memories of Union Station", I have written a few of my own. I was a frequent traveler through Union Station between the years of 1934 and until the end of the war. In my early years I traveled to track meets in New York, Boston and other places in the United States and, from 1941 until the end of the war I traveled as a Special Agent of the F. B. I.

Union Station was a very important part of my life between the years of 1934 and 1940 for, at that time, I was a young athlete from Indiana University traveling to the big track meets in the east almost every weekend from September to June. After my Friday classes at IU, I would take a bus to Indianapolis and get a train ticket to New York or wherever the track meet was being held. I would ride the day coach to Pittsburgh where I would get a "sleeper" on into New York. I would run my race on Saturday night, grab a train for Indianapolis and ride the day coach all the way to Indianapolis.

These trips provided me with money that I needed to continue my studies at IU, as well as giving me experience in running in the big track meets in the east. It was at these meets I was able to break world records and win national championships for the glory of IU and Indiana.

During those days, the A.A.U. had control over the athletes and no one received more money than his expense money to the meets. There was no advertising or side gifts, however, the athletes were allowed travel expenses. For example, on a trip to New York, I was allowed about $100.00 for the round trip. By riding the day coach half the way over and all of the way back, I was able to save almost half of my expense money. This was the way I managed to get through school. I knew every stop the train made, when it would take on water and coal, and even got acquainted with conductors and train personnel! They were my friends and they got to know my habits and even followed my races.

Indianapolis' Union Station was always a welcome place to come after a long and tiring trip. It was always clean and not crowded like the stations in New York and Boston. It was indeed a hub of travel in Indiana.

If I had extra time while waiting for a train, it was nice to look at the exhibits and to visit with other travelers.

In later years, as an F. B. I. Agent, I traveled to Washington D. C. and many other places in the United States by train. During the war years, Union Station was a very busy place, but still it was always clean and the personnel were friendly.

I have many fond memories of Union Station, and I am glad to see it being restored.

Respectfully yours,
DRL

* * *

TO: Mr. Michael Walter and Members of the Auburn, IN City Council
FROM: Donald R. Lash
DATE: August 18, 1992

I would like to take this opportunity to sincerely thank the members of the City Council of Auburn, Indiana and Norman Rohm, Mayor of Auburn, for adopting the resolution recommending that a park be named in my honor in there.

I would like to point out that my father was an orphan who came to Indiana on an "Orphan Train" from Boston, Massachusetts in 1898. There were six children in our family and my father worked at the Auburn Foundry as a molder and day laborer, while my mother cleaned homes to support our family.

Thanks to the City of Auburn and its wonderful, caring people, my parents were able to take care of this big family through the Depression years. We had a good school system and a community of churches whose members put out a helping hand to us. My teachers, as well as many of the people of Auburn whom I respected, encouraged me to continue my education.

Auburn is my hometown and will always be my hometown even though I do not reside there at the present time. Many of my early memories are from my days in Auburn.

I would like to challenge the young people growing up in Auburn to hold fast to the values that Auburn has always maintained, and to make the most of their lives so that some day, like myself, they will say, "Thank God I grew up, in Auburn, Indiana!"

Regards,
DRL

* * *

Don Lash as a State Representative

He Has Run The Last Long Mile
By Betty Killebrew
for the *Clintonian*, Clinton, Indiana

Let us honor one who's left us
At the end of life's hard test.
Let us dearly hold his memory
As he sleeps in well-earned rest.
He started life a country boy
Who would know the taste of fame.
But he never valued fame as much
As he valued his good name.
U.S. Champion in Cross-Country
For a record seven years,
A Sullivan award winner
Respected by his peers.
In the '36 Olympics
He ran for U.S. pride,
He served fellow man and country
From then until he died.
When we recall Don Lash's life
Some details to relate
Are his service to the F.B.I.
His college and his state.
He was a Christian and an athlete
A husband and a dad,
Who lived by the same principles
He grew by as a lad.
He began a Christian fellowship
He founded for our youth

And devoted many years of life
To spreading Christian truth.
His later life was simple
He was decent, he was clean,
As he stood four-square a pillar
On which local folks could lean.
But these facts of his obituary
Can't describe what he's attained
The peak of his accomplishment
Is the reward his soul has gained.
His memory will be sweeter
As the days grow into years
When we have quieted our grief
And have wiped away our tears.
For when we look behind us
And view his life, complete.
We'll be comforted by knowing,
That his death was not defeat.
The Christian hope he lived by,
Is assurance we can trust
That Don Lash will be there waiting
When we join him, as we must.
He has won the long hard contest,
He has run the last long mile,
He has passed across the finish line
And left us, for a while...

Message Delivered To Rockville, Indiana United Methodist Church, August, 1986

To the visitors with us this morning, let me say, "No, I'm sorry, but I am not Reverend Oaks. He advised me a few days ago that he had tried to get someone else to take his place today, but he was unable to get that person. I realized I was his last hope. And so, as a Layman, I will do the best that I can this morning.

The scripture was, of course, from the Old Testament, Judges 6:1-10. When I asked Rev. Oaks what I should talk about this morning, he said, "Whatever is on your heart!" I've thought about this and find I keep asking myself again and again, "How much longer will God continue to bless America before he loses His temper with us, and unleashes his wrath upon us?" God punished Israel many times in the Old Testament, and what makes America so different from Israel that we think we can avoid His wrath? I realize that the only time a whale is harpooned is when he is spouting, and so I will not try to spout this morning! However, I do wish to share with you my concerns for America.

In life, I am a realist. In the athletic world, I've found that we always have to pay the price when we do not do things right. Having read the Bible several times and believing firmly in the word of God, I am convinced that we have to pay for our sins and indiscretions.

I could have used a number of texts from the Old Testament to try and explain to you what I am trying to say this morning, because the Old Testament is filled with stories of the Israelites sinning in the sight of God and being punished by God again and again.

The very reasons the Israelites wandered for forty years after God had Moses lead them out of Egypt, was because they had sinned and had failed to keep God's commandments. From the very beginning when God created man, He spoke to man and He has continued speaking to him down through the ages. His commandments to us are very clear, and Christ, the son of God, has also spoken to man of sin and its consequences. Christ's disciples spoke on this subject again and again, and, even today, men of God are trying to reach us and get us to change our ways. It is fine to speak of love, and certainly Christ's life was one of love, but the Bible also speaks just as many times of punishment when we disobey God.

I dare say that today there is very little sin or crime committed by man which is done through ignorance of lack of knowledge on the subject. It would seem that God has created in us, deep down inside, a small voice which tells us right from wrong. This is the reason we should obey the law, because we already know what is right and should follow God's, as well as man's laws. But for some reason, just like Adam in the Garden of Eden, when God approached Adam after he had eaten of the fruit of the forbidden tree, Adam started to justify himself .. to alibi and to blame someone else for his sin. As you recall, Adam blamed Eve. This is still the case in America today.

Of course, Karl Marx, the father of Communism, for the sake of Communism, declared there was no God. Marx was also one who looked down on women. However, during his last days on earth, he was seen kneeling at his mother's grave sobbing. Even Karl Marx knew right from wrong. Even though he declared there was no God to the Communists, he knew in the end that God does exist.

I spent 21 years in the F.B.I. interviewing criminals and taking statements from most of them. They all knew they had sinned in the sight of God, and, just like Adam, they all tried to alibi and blame someone else because of their sin or crime. They all told me it was never their fault! Yet, almost everyone of them admitted they were glad they had been caught and that their time of running from the law was over.

God has blessed America as no other nation in the world. I doubt if even the Israelites, God's chosen people, have enjoyed more blessings than has America. Perhaps it is because America was founded by God fearing men and women. But in spite of all of the blessings God has given America, we seem to be sliding farther and farther from the laws that God laid down for His people. My question this morning is, "How much longer will God bless America before He loses his temper and unleashes His wrath upon us?" What makes America so different from Israel that we can avoid His wrath? A thousand years is but a day in the sight of God and this country is not even a thousand years old yet. Most of us love our country, and we have been loyal to it and served it in many, ways. Naturally, we have concerns for it and our concerns are many. It is the American people themselves who have become the problem. We can alibi for our drug problems today by saying it is the fault of the "pusher", the "importers", or the "foreign countries". but the problem in narcotics today is with our own people. if there was no demand for narcotics in America, there would be no market for it.

Some of the fundamentals we have stood for in this country, like freedom of the press (which we must have to remain a free nation) have been taken advantage of today. Smut is printed, advertisements are permitted that destroy us, and false reports are made in order to sell news copy.

Recently, for the first time in American history, an F.B.I. Agent and a C.I.A. Agent sold their country for "twenty pieces of silver". Last week, the murder rate in Indianapolis averaged nearly one a day. The list goes on and on in today's paper.

It was unfortunate recently that one of our well-known university athletes, a basketball player, became involved in the drug problem. This not only degraded him, but also his university. He tried drugs for the first time, but it was one time too many and it cost him his life.

I have always defended athletics, because much good has been accomplished through sports when young people learn to discipline themselves. In sports, our youth can create opportunities for themselves and others. It is my opinion that athletics should be used as a means to an end, a means to get an education or a means to get ahead in the world, and not as an end in itself. Few athletes go on to make their living in athletics.

I received many awards: the Sullivan Award, Hall of Fame, All-American, etc., but every time I received an award, God extracted from me a responsibility. This was a responsibility to my people and to the young boys and girls who would follow or even to one who might look up to me and try to follow in my footsteps.

I have been out of athletics for a long time: fifty years. But I find that my deeds follow me even today. Not long ago, a reporter for Sports Illustrated contacted me and stated that they were about to do a story on a young man who had already won three national championships in cross country and was going for this fourth. Upon checking the record books, they found that Don Lash had won seven consecutive national championships in cross country. So, you see, our deeds do follow us!

The problem in athletics today is like the problem in many other lines of work: we have a few people who think only of themselves. They forget that others are looking to them for an example; they forget they are responsible to these younger athletes. Some universities have used the athletes to build the universities. In professional athletics, some cities and promoters have tried to enrich themselves. In order to do this, they have had to bid outlandish prices for the professional skills of some athletes. What athlete is worth several million dollars in one season? You and I know what one dollar means to us and how hard some work for so little. It is hard to think of them earning millions in one season. I am certain that if the big money was not there, many of the professional athletes who have gotten into trouble would not be there in the first place.

I have only scratched the surface this morning of the problems of this country. What about the home and the example that parents set before their children? What about our businesses in some cases? Are all of the lawsuits necessary or are some people just trying to get something for nothing? What about the business or insurance fraud today? What about the irresponsible politician? Is it his fault or is it ours for not learning how he his voted in the past and how he has performed while holding other public offices? Should we vote him out of office'?

Again, my question this morning is, "How much longer will God hold His wrath from a nation who has not kept His commandments?" First Corinthians, 12: 31 says, "...I will show you a more excellent way. " America is truly carrying a great burden and it is getting heavier. There certainly is a more excellent way! If America does not turn back to God, as our Founding Fathers did in establishing America, we will soon be lost as a nation!

I know a young man who is well-educated, well-read, and very knowledgeable. He served his country in the armed forces and is concerned about the atom bomb which, no doubt, he should be. To protect himself, he has built himself a bomb shelter in his backyard. He has stocked it with food and knows exactly how many people it will hold: his family. He feels he is preparing for the future. I too, am aware of the atom bomb and know the intent of the Communist party to "communize" the world. I don't know if a bomb shelter could save my life or not in case the bomb falls, but I feel that, as a Christian, I don't really don't care. What would life be like if I did survive under these conditions? Rather than an earthly shelter, I have put my faith in my Lord Jesus Christ. For, without Christ, life is meaningless.

Some people feel the Old Testament was for the old Israel. The New Testament is for the modern world. May I read from the New Testament this morning.? Matthew 24: 32 says, "Now learn this lesson from the fig tree: as soon as its twigs get tender and its leaves come out, you know that summer is near." Like the fig tree, when it puts on its leaves, we know summer is near. With crime so rampant in America, is judgment near? A thousand years is but a day to God. When will God punish our nation? This I do not know, but this much I do know: God has said that He will punish the wicked. Thanks be to God and His son, Jesus, we can repent of our sins as a nation, and, as individuals, we can change our ways and live to see God in all of His glory!

* * *

News Release To Parke County, Indiana Area Newspapers From Lash Realty

Don and Margaret Lash were guests of Ohio State University in Columbus, Ohio May 6th through May 8th to take part in ceremonies dedicating the new Jesse Owens Track & Field Facility on the Ohio State campus. The Lashes attended a number of receptions which were given for members of the 1936 Olympic Team which had included Jesse Owens. This was the first reunion for members of the '36 Team since the ticker-tape parade in New York City immediately after their return.

One of the things which makes the '36 Olympics important in history is that it was the first modern Olympics and was shrouded in politics. Adolph Hitler had just come into power and was determined to use the Olympic Games to showcase the superiority of the German people He wanted to show the world that Germany had recovered from World War I and survived through the depression. Hitler had spent 30 million dollars on the facilities alone, thus making the Berlin games the start of the modern Olympics in terms of capital spending.

Lash stated that there has been much controversy surrounding the '36 Olympics centering around Jesse Owens and other black athletes. However, those attending the reunion were in agreement on several things: first, the games were not the propaganda success in favor of Hitler and his party that he had hoped they would be; second, the games were in themselves, however, a great success and every member of the American team was treated with respect and courtesy; third, the German people, as a whole, adored Jesse Owens and the black athletes who performed. As Mack Robinson, a black athlete and silver medalist behind Jesse Owens (and the older brother of Jackie Robinson, the first black athlete to cross the color line in major league baseball) stated, "The blacks on the U.S. Team were actually treated better in the '36 Olympics than they were back home in the United States."

As for Hitler, Lash stated, "We as a team refused to salute Hitler during the Olympic parade around the oval track, and I still feel that this was as it should have been. However, it should be remembered that Hitler stated before the games that he would not and could not possibly recognize all of the first place athletes from around the world during the Olympic games. There is no doubt but what he was a sports enthusiast and naturally did honor the winners of his own country."

Like Hitler, other countries have tried to use the Olympic Games as a political football. In 1936, Russia refused to compete saying that until the world was completely Communistic, Russia would not compete in the Olympics. Since then they have chosen to use the games for propaganda reasons. In 1980, our own country refused to compete for political reasons. Lash stated that he feels that, "Politics should be deleted completely from the Olympic Games and decisions should be left to the athletes, the coaches and the National and International Olympic bodies to determine when a team will or will not compete."

Lash says, "The reunion in Columbus was a great privilege" and that he personally was interested in each athlete and what that athlete had been able to accomplish in his life because of athletics. He stated that most of the athletes had used their athletic background as a means of opportunity and not an end in itself. Doors had been opened to most of them and they had lived successful lives. Perhaps the most disappointed ones were those who had used athletics as an end in itself and could bask in the sunshine of their accomplishments only for a short time. Lash noted that most retired athletes are like other senior citizens: they like to be recognized, occasionally get on TV, and have their stories printed. He adds that when the former Olympians saw the new Jesse Owens Track, some were overheard to say, "If we had had a track like this, our records would never have been broken!" Lash commented, "They seem to forget that when a record is set, it becomes a goal for someone else and it will be broken."

Lash stated that perhaps the biggest joke to himself was when one of the former athletes said to him "Don, you are the only one who looks in good shape and has not gained over one hundred pounds!" He admitted that with five heart by-passes, he would not even make it around the first turn of the track. He also said he realized that if any more medals were to be given, they should go to the spouses who put up with old record holders who attend athletic reunions.

❊ ❊ ❊

Donald R. Lash Fact Sheet

Born
• August 15, 1912, Bluffton, Indiana

Married
• June 18, 1938 to Margaret Mendenhall Lash

Children
• Three children: Russell, David and Marguerite
• Nine grandchildren
• Two great-grandchildren

Died
• September 19, 1994, resident of Rockville, Indiana

Education
• Attended Auburn, Indiana grade school and high school, graduating 1933
• Received B.S. and M.S. degrees from Indiana University, Bloomington, Indiana

Athletics
• While a student at Auburn High School, coached by Zeke Young, was State Champion in Mile and Half-Mile Runs
• Ran track and cross country at Indiana University under coach E.C. Hayes where he broke world records in two mile runs indoors and outdoors. Anchored medley and four-mile relay teams to world records. First American to run two-miles under nine minutes.
• National Cross Country Champion for seven consecutive years: a record that stood for 50 years
• Member, 1936 U.S. Olympic Team to Berlin, Germany, competing in the 5,000 and 10,000 meter events
• Held every national record from 3,000 to 10,000 meters in 1935, 1936 and 1937
• Received the James E. Sullivan Award in 1938 as the most outstanding amateur athlete in the U.S.
• Member, U.S. Track Hall of Fame
• Member, A.A.U. Track & Field Hall of Fame (awarded posthumously, 1995)
• Member, State of Indiana Track Hall of Fame
• Charter member, Indiana University Hall of Fame

Careers
• Served three years, Indiana State Police
• Served 21 years, Special Agent and firearms expert for the F.B.I
• Served five terms (10 years), Indiana General Assembly
• Served 2-1/2 years, Trustee, Indiana University
• Served ten years, Fellowship of Christian Athletes (F.C.A.) National Staff and served as first Regional Director for F.C.A.
• Founder and operator of Camp Wapello, a Christian camp for youth near Marshall, Indiana, now the National Resource and Training F.C.A.
• Awarded "Sagamore of the Wabash" by Indiana Governor Otis R. Bowen, the highest award presented in Indiana to those who have rendered distinguished service to the state in 1979
• Founder, Don Lash Realtors, Rockville, Indiana in 1973
• Served as President, Vermilion County (Indiana) Hospital Foundation

Biographical Data Prepared For Indiana University By David R. Lash, Ed.D.

Donald Ray Lash received his B.S. Degree in 1938 in Physical Education and his M. S. Degree in Law Enforcement in 1940 from Indiana University. While an undergraduate student at IU, he became a member of the 1936 Olympic team, broke the world's record in the two-mile run both indoors and outdoors, anchored I. U.'s medley and 4-mile relay teams to world records and won numerous national championships in track and cross country. He won three National Cross Country Championships while at IU and continued running to win a total of seven consecutive Cross Country Championships. This record stood for fifty years which is a record in itself.

While at IU, he received the L.G. Balfour Award in 1935-36-37, the Jake Gimbel Award, and the prestigious James E. Sullivan Award which is given annually for the most outstanding amateur athlete in the United States.

He enrolled in the first class of Police Science which was offered at the University. Upon receiving his B.S. degree he became a member of the Indiana State Police, and, as an officer, spoke before numerous schools and service clubs throughout the State of Indiana. He was a firm believer in crime prevention and felt it was more important to prevent crime than to solve the crime after the fact.

In 1941 he left the State Police to become a Special Agent of the Federal Bureau of Investigation (F.B.I.). He became a firearms expert and a police school instructor. Don traveled throughout the United States, speaking before police departments and teaching in their schools. Lash also worked on some of the Bureau's most important criminal cases and was rated as one of that agency's top agents. He retired from the Bureau in 1963 after twenty one years of service.

While with the F.B.I., he and his family purchased 60 acres in Parke County, Indiana and started a non-profit Christian camp called "Camp Wapello" for young people. After retirement from the F.B.I., he became the first Regional Director of the Fellowship of Christian Athletes (F.C.A.) in the United States. He formed what is termed "Huddle Groups" for the F.C.A. in many schools throughout the country.

In 1971, the F. C. A. took over ownership of the 350-acre camp, and Don continued on as a fund raiser for the organization. Today the camp is known as the National Resource and Training Center for the F.C.A., and young people come there from all over the country for the organization's national conferences. The camp is complete with a church and many athletic facilities, including one building which houses four basketball courts. This camp is an outgrowth of the desire Don had to provide a Christian camping environment for young people.

Don served as an elected Trustee of Indiana University and in the Indiana General Assembly as a State Representative for ten years. He also served in many public service capacities. In 1965, he was chairman of the American Heart Association Campaign Fund in Marion County, Indiana, and he was the first chairman of the Vermilion County Hospital Foundation from 1983-1987. In 1974, he received the Clevenger Award from IU, in 1979 he was named a "Sagamore of the Wabash" by Indiana Governor Otis R. Bowen, and in 1985 he received the Jefferson Award for distinguished service granted by the Indianapolis STAR Newspaper. He was in the first group to be inducted into the IU Intercollegiate Athletic Hall of Fame.

Until his death from cancer in 1994, he was a Broker with Don Lash Realtors, which he founded in 1974. Shortly before his death, he was instrumental in obtaining the housing for the Parke County Health and Help Center.

Lash served as President of the Parke County Historical Society from 1985 to 1989. During that time, and under his direction, an updated historical book of Parke County was written. He also served on the boards of Billie Creek Village, a historical re-creation of turn-of-the-century Parke County, and Parke County, Inc., an organization dedicated to the economic development of the western-Indiana community.

Don spent a good deal of his life in crime prevention and trying to better the lives of his fellow Americans. His motto for life, and one which is engraved on his headstone, reads: "The older I become, the more I am convinced that true happiness comes from helping others."

※ ※ ※

True Stories and Cock-'n-Bull Stories
My Dad
By Marguerite Lash Klausmeier

Dad was the first and one of the best story tellers I ever knew. As a little girl growing up in our big old house on Layman Avenue in Indianapolis, I'd curl up with him and ask for a story. Inevitably, his question to me was always same, "All right, Marguerite, now do you want a TRUE story? Or, do you want a COCK-'N-BULL story,?" Then I had to decide which I wanted and usually the latter type of stories won out, because they were the most fun! Actually, I don't think he had that large a repertoire of stories, but somehow I never tired of listening to them. And the really amazing part is that today my kids remember that he always kept the details of even the cock-'n-bull stories the same!

I would like to apologize to Mrs. Meininger, my first grade teacher at Indianapolis Public School #57. One day I fully upset her class when she made the fatal error of asking, "Children, what kind of story would you like to hear today?" It just seemed natural to me to blurt out, "A cock-'n-bull story! " That night my mother got a call that began, "Mrs. Lash, would you please tell Marguerite NOT to request cock-'n-bull stories in my class anymore?"

Presented below are a few of dad's stories. These represent a collection of the ones recalled by family and friends and the ones he wrote down near the end of his life. The reader can decide which parts are true and which parts are "cock-'n-bull". As you read, note the number of times he, in a tongue in cheek remark, says, "The devil must have spoken to me when I did that!"

And now, as Don Lash would say, "Do you want a true story or a cock-'n-bull story?"

* * *

> ## My Dad
> ## By Marguerite Lash Klausmeier
> **Written December, 1981**
>
> If you don't know my Dad,
> Then you're missing a lot
> Of what makes a life worth living.
>
> He is quick with a smile,
> He can laugh all the while,
> And his whole life is based upon giving.
>
> I've seen him mad,
> I've seen him sad
> I've seen him handle trouble.
>
> But even the things that get
> You and me down,
> Have never burst his bubble.
>
> There is no doubt
> Within my mind,
> That when Dad has gone to Glory,
>
> The angels will be waiting
> On him, to tell them a
> "Cock and Bull' story.

One of my younger sisters, Isabelle, had a favorite cat. As a boy, I became impressed with seeing a man jump out of an airplane with a parachute. I finally convinced Isabelle that a cat could successfully use a parachute if a handkerchief was fastened to the cat and it were dropped from a higher elevation. Everything went fine until I dropped her cat from the barn roof. It immediately grabbed the strings and the parachute deflated. I yelled, "Parachute didn't open!" and my sister became hysterical. The cat did land on its feet as I had described to Isabelle, but without the use of the parachute, which had become deflated. The cat landed with a big thud, and, fortunately, the cat must have had more thin one life because it lived. I was severely reprimanded!

* * *

My father and I used to enjoy shooting a BB gun at a cake of soap in the kitchen during the long winter nights. One evening I recall that I shot at the cake of soap and it fell over. My dad went forth and stooped over to set the cake of soap back to an upright position. The devil must have spoken to me at that moment, for I shot him on the part of his body where he usually sat down! He immediately jumped up and screamed and ran into my mother, pulled his pants down and said, "Old woman can you see any blood?" (My dad, Brandon Lash, frequently called my mother, Pearl, "old woman".) Mother said, "No, but there is a big red spot!" My dad threatened to thrash the daylights out of me, but, strange as it may seem, my father never spanked me. It was always my mother who spanked me. In this case, she was not involved, and so I was spared the spanking I so richly deserved!

On another occasion. when I was a freshman in high school I had brought my track pants and shirt home to be washed. I had placed them in a kettle and was boiling them on the stove. The shirt was red and the water was about the color of cocoa. My dad came in and asked, "Is that cocoa on the stove?" Again, the devil must have spoken to me, and I said, "Sure, it's cocoa!" Dad then proceeded to pour some of the water into a cup and take a big drink. He said, "It doesn't taste like cocoa!" I said, "Oh, no! That's my sweat clothes being washed!" Again, I was threatened, but never punished.

* * *

My poor sister Josephine was the oldest child in our family and suffered many embarrassments when she started dating. I, along with my brother Charles and other sisters would often peek in the windows or hide behind the furniture to hear and see what went on with her dates. Then, at the family dinner table a full report would be made in front of everyone. On one occasion, Josephine got so mad at me for embarrassing her that she started throwing dinner plates at me. I remember running out of the door and one plate had been thrown with such force that it was rolling past me faster than I could run!

I recall one of her dates was a man who was losing his hair prematurely. Charles and I decided to end this companionship very quickly! So we went out and pushed his Model-T Ford way down the road where we then hid it in the woods. When Josephine and her friend went out to take a little joy ride, the car was no where to be found. I understood later that the car was reported stolen, but, after a thorough search the following day, the car was found. Of course, my brother and I "knew nothing about it" and acted horrified that such a thing could happen!

Sunday was an important day at our house, because after church we would have a big dinner. Frequently my mother would invite the preacher.

The preacher would always take my mother and father up on their hospitality, but somehow I don't think he liked me very well! I was just a sweet, innocent little boy!

I remember one of these Sundays when the preacher was visiting and we all went out to the pump to wash up for dinner. Now as our preacher was washing up, he happened to remove his false teeth and set them down beside the pump. It just so happened that we had killed a hog the day before and the hog's teeth were laying nearby. The devil must have spoken to me, and I switched the preacher's false teeth and the hog's teeth. When the preacher put the hog's teeth in his mouth, he started talking like a pig!!

Immediately my mother knew that I had been up to something! "Donald!," she yelled. (I don't know why, but she always called me "Donald!") She immediately sent me to my room as punishment. The preacher's teeth were found and returned to him.

So many times when the preacher showed up, I was sent to my room! Since I didn't want to miss out on these wonderful Sunday dinners, I knew what to do whenever this happened! You see, my room just happened to be over the dinner table, and so I had drilled a hole in the floor just the right size through which to pull my dinner! When the preacher went to say grace...and fortunately, he always said long prayers...I'd whip out my fishing pole and carefully lower the line through the hole in my floor. Then I'd whip up a chicken leg to the safety of my room! Next, I'd snag a biscuit! One time I even got a whole pitcher of milk! All the while, my entire family and the preacher would sit around the table giving thanks with eyes closed and heads bowed, and no one would notice me sneaking food from my perch overhead! Then when the preacher finally said, "Amen!" everyone would look up, and my mother would say, "I thought I made more chicken than that!" By that time, I'd closed the hole back up and no one would be the wiser!

※ ※ ※

I think the thing, I enjoyed the most growing up was our large family. We often had our squabbles, but we always pulled together. In those days there was no TV, but we did have an Atwater Kent radio which would operate slightly if we took the battery out of the Model-T Ford for electrical power and used the clothesline as an aerial.

The old Model-T Fords that we drove were always secondhand, and they cost around $25 to $30.00. Whenever the whole family went anywhere we could barely squeeze in, and Isabelle always had to sit on Charles' lap as there was no room for her to sit down. He always referred to her as "razor butt", because she was thin and her bones were sharp on his legs.

On one such occasion we were all piled into the Model-T going from Auburn to Bluffton to visit my grandparents. As we proceeded through the small town of Ossian, I stuck my head up through a hole in the top of the car and waved at people all along the route. Father didn't notice what I was doing and said, "My goodness! This is a very friendly town! I'm amazed at how many people are waving at us!" He was not aware that people were merely returning my wave!

* * *

Due to the fact that I was a good hunter and usually got my game on the first shot, others liked to hunt with me. We had a neighbor by the name of Howard Emmy, and we enjoyed hunting together. I recall going hunting one morning and I had shot fourteen rabbits. Howard ended up with none. His parents were gone that day and his mother had a small flock of chickens. He wanted to impress his mother with his hunting ability and asked me if I would exchange rabbits for chickens. I decided that chickens were better eating than rabbits, so we shot the heads off of fourteen chickens and he took the rabbits. That evening, his mother went out to feed the chickens, and half of her flock was missing! Howard told his mother about the exchange of rabbits for chickens. He received a hard spanking, and I had chicken for dinner!!

I used to love to hunt squirrels. A neighbor, Mr. Evans, had a very fine woods with lots of squirrels, but he allowed no hunting on the property. I would often slip into his woods and wait until two or three squirrels were out playing. I would shoot in rapid succession: getting my squirrels and getting out of the woods quickly before Evans was able to catch me! Evans got to hiding in the woods hoping to catch me. Fortunately, his property was northwest of our property, and the prevailing winds, were usually from the northwest. Evans didn't realize it, but he frequently smoked a pipe and I caught the smell of his pipe when he was hiding in the woods, and thus I always knew his location. I often aggravated him by pretending as if I were going to climb the fence and go onto his property, but I always withdrew when he was nearby. I recall of him telling another neighbor that he was going to catch me (he called me the "little bastard"), but for some "unknown" reason, I would never get on his property when he was laying for me!

* * *

As a family, we struggled to make a living. Our main crops were onions and potatoes. One of every two or three years, we would raise sugar cane and make sorghum molasses. When I was about eight years old, the only place to get the water squeezed out of the cane and made into molasses was in Ohio, about forty miles away. We had gone over in the Model-T Ford and found the place. Several days later, we had a wagon load of sugar cane with the leaves stripped off and ready to be made into molasses. Since everyone was busy, I volunteered to drive a team of horses with a load of sugar cane. It was an all day trip, and when I got to the cane camp darkness had begun to fall. The owner of the camp insisted I stay all night. When I did not arrive home that evening, my mother was very concerned. The following day, however, I did return. She often spoke of her concern on this situation.

* * *

Grandfather Landis lost his arm in a thrashing machine accident. The arm had been replaced with a metal hook. He had a very bad temper, and I can remember that when he got mad, we all had to duck, because he'd swing that hook at us!

On the other hand, Grandfather Lash didn't have the same temperament as Grandpa Landis. I loved to go out and visit my Grandmother and Grandfather Lash on their farm, and they loved having me there. However, one of the few spankings I ever remember getting was when I was about three or four years old. I hid from my grandmother (as small children do when they are playing) and after several hours of looking for me, she became frantic. She rang the dinner bell which was used only in case of danger or fire. I recall my grandfather running in out of the field and several neighbors coming down. At this point, I made my appearance, and it was one of the few spankings I ever received.

* * *

When I was in about the second grade, several Civil War veterans still lived in our community. One such veteran lived in the house behind ours and told me many stories about the Civil War. Another Civil War veteran, named McIntosh, often visited the school and told many Civil War stories. Our high school in Auburn was named after him.

I barely remember World War I, but I vividly recall the signing of the Armistice and the end of that war. They had a parade in Auburn and my father drove the Auburn Foundry truck in the parade. (Auburn Foundry was where he was employed at that time.) Years later, when I was in high school, one of the World War I aviators would fly over the Auburn football field and drop a football with red and black ribbons (the school colors) onto the field to be used in the game.

* * *

I remember one dark night around Halloween when I was about ten years old, several of us kids were out walking in Auburn. As we passed a cemetery, we could hear a voice calling out from behind one of the tombstones and it seemed to be counting, "One for you and one for me ... and one for you and one for me." We all came to the conclusion that it must be God and the devil dividing up souls! "One for you and one for me," the voice continued. All of a sudden another voice spoke up from behind a tombstone and said, "Careful! I hear some kids coming! Do you want to get them or should I?" We all lit out of there as fast as our little legs could carry us! We didn't want to find out what would happen next!

The next day we found out that the local bank had been robbed just the night before. Apparently what we heard was the bank robbers counting out the money, "One for you and one for me..."

* * *

Because of my talents in running, I was frequently called upon to chase criminals on foot, both in the Indiana State Police and while in the FBI. During World War II while I was stationed in Birmingham, Alabama, we frequently had to go out and bring in moonshiners and draft dodgers. On one particular occasion, we had to go out into the mountains and get a draft dodger. The other agents and I knew his family would try to protect him, and so they let me out of the car at the bottom of the hill out of sight from the cabin where the man lived with his family. I was to run up the backside of the hill and catch him if he came out the back door. The other agents would go up to the cabin, knock on the front door, and ask for him.

So they proceeded up the front of the mountain while I ran up the back way and hid behind a tree just outside the house. Sure enough, when the agents arrived and asked about the man, his family said he wasn't there. And as we expected, as they walked up to the front door, out he ran through the back door! I caught him and marched him around to the front just as his family was denying his whereabouts.

On another occasion, I was stationed with the Bureau in Indianapolis. We had word that a bank robbery suspect was staying at a motel out on East Washington Street. Apparently, the suspect was watching for me from his room, because, when I went to the motel office to inquire about the suspect and which room he was in, he ran out of the room, jumped in his convertible, and took off at high speed out east on U.S. 40. I immediately jumped in my car and took off after him. I was alone when this happened.

As the suspect drove off, I knew I had to stop him or else he would kill someone with his car. In the Bureau we were taught you never pull your gun unless you plan to kill someone, but, in twenty-one years with the FBI, I never shot anyone even though I was a firearms expert. So I decided to give this suspect a scare. The top was down on his car, and I pulled my gun and aimed about five feet over his head. Going about 65 miles per hour, I knew that bullet would really zing by his head and he'd hear it! But instead of stopping, he scooted down into his seat and went faster! So I shot at him again, and this time I aimed about two feet lower! This time he stopped and did just what I was hoping he would do! He pulled off to the side of the road and he began to run! I started to chase him on foot, but I pretended that I couldn't quite catch him! I let him run for a couple of miles, before I finally ran up and grabbed him. At this point, he fell exhausted on the ground.

I just couldn't resist having a little fun with him after all this, and so I asked him, "Brother, have I made a Christian out of you yet?" Lying there on the ground and trying to catch his breath, he looked up at me and said, "A Christian? Man, you nearly made an angel out of me back there!"

* * *

My work in law enforcement often took me into some unusual places to look for suspects. I remember one time we went into a farmhouse looking for a couple of suspects, but we couldn't find them anywhere. Going out the back door, we checked the outbuilding and found the two men hiding in the chicken coop! They were covered with feathers and chicken droppings!

Don's Last Known Running Race
By Dave Lash

During the summer of 1957, my father, Don Lash, and I were working near the lake at Camp Wapello in Parke County, Indiana. Dad had bought an old used black 1940 Chevrolet sedan that he let me refer to as "Dave's car" to be used at the camp. I had driven the car down to the earthen dam with tools in it while we cut brush together. Mon had been busy back at the cabin keeping house and making lunch for us.

Suddenly, Dad challenged me to a running race against the old car. Dad said that he could out run my old car in a race back to the cabin for lunch. My pride was too much for me with my old car to be beaten by my father in such a race. Dad had wisely noticed that the car was turned in the wrong direction and that by the time I could get it turned around he would have a "head start" on me. I quickly took Dad up on the challenge. Dad, hot and tired, dressed in track pants, t-shirt and tennis shoes, took off running cross country. He made a straight path through rough brush, briars and tall weeds back towards the cabin. I raced the old car back the curved lake road towards the cabin in only 1st and 2nd gears holding the accelerator to the floorboard. I was determined not to get beat by the old champion runner who had beaten me many times before. I remember coming to the intersection of the main road that ran back to the cabin. I reared the old car up on one side on 2 wheels while skidding around the corner with the engine running wide open. Dad was well out in front. I could see a long way up the road and Dad's legs were churning in the wind as we approached the cabin.

My car was quickly catching up with Dad when suddenly both of us saw a bicycle parked sideways in the middle of the narrow one lane road lined with pine trees. Mom had parked the bike in the road to keep me from driving the car up around the cabin and making lots of dust. I jammed the brakes as hard as I could as the car skidded to a sliding halt right up to the bike. Dad raced right around the bike on up to the cabin to be the winner. I stopped the car, jumped out, threw the bike out of the road, jumped back in the old car and raced on up to the cabin. There at the door of the cabin was mom mad at all the dust and Dad laughing with that boyish grin with yet another win to his credit.

Epilogue
By Marguerite Lash Klausmeier

We buried dad on September 23, 1994. I remember standing at the grave site after everyone had left, and the cemetery workers were politely waiting as I, the last one standing near the casket, gazed at the beautiful oak coffin that just a few minutes before was decorated with an Olympic flag and a spray of red roses. I commented to the workers that dad's life had been, "Pretty good...in fact, not bad for a poor Indiana farm boy." They agreed. Dad's life was a tribute to all the good things we hold dear as Americans: someone from humble beginnings can still rise in our society and become a success. Moreover, his life was a testimony that when we commit our lives to God and submit our will to His, He will protect our steps and accomplish great things through us.

Index

A
A.A.U. Track & Field Hall of Fame 7, 45
Amateur Sports Center of the United States 52
American Heart Association 62
American Red Cross 32
Auburn High School 9, 10, 45
Auburn Star 9

B
Balfour, L.G. 48, 61
Beech Nut Chewing Gum Company 13, 17
Biederman, Carol 31
Book Nook 43
Borns, Frank 53
Boston Garden 16
Bowen, Otis R. 36, 45, 62
Brown, Tarzan 48

C
Camp Wapello 27, 30, 31, 41, 45, 61, 69
Cavinder, Fred D. 50
Chicago Relays 18
Clevenger, Z.G. 48
Clintonian 42
Cripe, C.C. 38
Cunningham, Glen 16, 19

D
Deckard, Tommy 13, 14, 16
Delta Chi Fraternity 17
Dill 5, 6

E
Evans 66

F
F.C.A. 34
Federal Bureau of Investigation 6, 19, 25, 30, 32, 34, 38, 42, 44, 45, 50, 51, 57, 61, 68
Fellowship of Christian Athletes 20, 45, 49, 61

G
Guidone, Joe 28

H
Harvard University 5
Hayes, Billy 17
Hayes, E. C. 5, 10, 13, 16, 19, 45, 48
Hayes, Helen 52
Hitler 59, 60
Hoover, J. Edgar 6, 37, 38

I
Indiana State Police 18
Indiana General Assembly 34
Indiana State Museum 14
Indiana State Police 6, 18, 45, 61, 68
Indiana Track Hall of Fame 7
Indiana United Methodist Church 56
Indiana University 5, 6, 12, 13, 17, 18, 32, 36, 38, 43, 45, 61
Indiana University Hall of Fame 7, 45
Indianapolis Star Newspaper 50, 62
Irvington Methodist 27
IU Intercollegiate Athletic Hall of Fame 62
IU Memorial Union 48

J
Jarrett, Eleanor Holm 52
Jesse Owens Track 60
Jesse Owens Track & Field Facility 59
Johnston, Roe 32
Jones, Bobby 51

K
Killebrew, Betty 42

L
Landis 67
Landis, Daniel 7
Landis, Pearl 7
Lash, Anna 7, 8
Lash, Brandon 7, 47, 64
Lash, Charles 6, 7, 8, 10, 64
Lash, David 19, 29, 32, 34, 37, 45, 69
Lash, Elizabeth 37
Lash, Jean 47
Lash, Josephine 8, 64
Lash, Margaret 19, 22, 25, 29, 30, 34, 37, 41, 43, 45
Lash, Marguerite 25, 29, 32, 37, 45, 62, 63, 70
Lash, Pearl 7
Lash Realtors Company 34, 45, 49, 62
Lash, Russell 19, 29, 32, 37, 44, 45
Lease, Jim 17
Lilly Endowment 33
Little Church Around the Corner 18, 43
Lynn, John 33

M
Madison Square Garden 16
Marx, Karl 57
McCartney, Bill 31
McFadden 22
Medcalfe, Larry 41
Memorial Hall 17
Mendenhall, Charlotte 17
Miller, Sam 17
Miller, Tom J. 47
Model-T Ford 65, 66
Morris, Glen 52

71

N

National Fellowship of Christian Athletes 32
New York Athletic Club 14
New York Sports Writers 5
Nurmi, Paavo 13

O

Oaks 56
Ohio State University 59
Owens, Jesse 59

P

Parke County Health and Help Center 62
Parke County Historical Society 38, 62
Pearl Harbor 19
Penn Relays 16
Petty, Harvey 27
Princeton Invitational Meet 18
Princeton University 11, 13
Purdue University 10, 46

R

Randall's Island 13

Ridgefarm Friends Church 30, 41
Robinson, Jackie 60
Robinson, Mack 60
Robinson, Sid 5, 6
Rohm, Norman 54
Romani, Archie San 19
Romoser, Dale 31

S

Saturday Evening Post 9
Sewell, Jane 41
Smith, Jimmy 16
Sports Illustrated 5, 13, 48
State of Indiana Track Hall of Fame 45
Sugar Bowl Football Game 14, 18
Sugar Bowl Meet 14, 18
Sugar Creek 28, 31
Sullivan 42, 50, 52, 58
Sullivan, James E. 7, 14, 45, 51, 61
Sunrise Drive 18

T

Tech High School 46

Trutt, Mel 16
Turkey Run State Park 32

U

U.S. Track Hall of Fame 7, 45
Union Station 53
US Army 30

V

Vermilion County Hospital 38, 45, 62
Veterans Hospital 20

W

Walter, Michael 54
Wapello 26, 33, 41

Y

Y.M.C.A. 6, 32, 33
Young, Violet 38
Young, Zeke 6, 9, 38, 45

Z

Zamperini 14